LANDMARKS OF
SAN FRANCISCO

LANDMARKS OF

SAN FRANCISCO

PATRICK MCGREW

ORIGINAL PHOTOGRAPHY BY

MARION BRENNER

HARRY N. ABRAMS, INC., PUBLISHERS, NEW YORK

FOR JONATHAN MALONE

Editor: Mark Greenberg
Designer: Bob McKee

Library of Congress Cataloging-in-Publication Data
McGrew, Patrick.
Landmarks of San Francisco / Patrick McGrew ;
photography by Marion Brenner.
p.   cm.
Includes index.
ISBN 0-8109-3557-0 (cloth)
1. Historic buildings—California—San Francisco—Guide-books.
2. Historic districts—California—San Francisco—Guide-books.
3. San Francisco (Calif.)—Buildings, structures, etc.—Guide-books.
4. San Francisco (Calif.)—Description—Guide-books.
I. Brenner, Marion.   II. Title.
F869.S38M37   1991
917.94′610453—dc20   90-24271
                                                                              CIP

Photograph Credits
Unless noted below, all photographs are by Marion Brenner.
Pages 20, 36-37, 158, 267: Patrick McGrew; page 140 Page & Turnbull;
page 214: courtesy Josef Betz; page 226 *rendering* by Whistler-Patri;
page 243: *rendering* by Kajima Associates and Whistler-Patri.

Frontispiece:
Mills Building and Tower
220 Montgomery Street and 220 Bush Street
Landmark Number 76
(commentary on page 118)

Contents

Acknowledgments 6

A Message from Mayor Art Agnos 7

Introduction 8

Landmarks of San Francisco 16

Appendices

I Historic Districts 286

II Designated Structures of Merit 293

III Downtown-Plan Protected Buildings 293

IV California Registered Historical Landmarks
and Points of Historical Interest in San Francisco 295

V Sites on the National Register of Historic
Places in San Francisco 296

Index 298

ACKNOWLEDGMENTS

Many people have contributed to this book directly or indirectly, including my mentor and predecessor on the Landmarks Board, Gee Gee Platt, and the secretary to the Board, the late Jonathan Malone. Others who deserve mention include former mayors George Moscone and Dianne Feinstein, former Supervisor Jack Molinari, and Alan Lubliner, Mary Burns, Betty Delosada, and Mark Ryser.

Special friends along the way who helped with the work and, consequently, the book include Jeremy Naploha and Pat Starrett. Allan Temko and Gerald Adams have proven to be invaluable friends, not only to me and this project but also to preservation in San Francisco. In New York, my friend Ned Bayrd and my editor at Abrams, Mark Greenberg, have given me the necessary confidence to complete this book, which has been fully realized in Bob McKee's fine design.

My assistant, Eric Smith, deserves acknowledgment, as does my best friend, Bob Stone, who always helps me set my sights higher.

Patrick McGrew

A Message from the Mayor of the City of San Francisco

Even for those of us who are privileged to live here, a book like *Landmarks of San Francisco* is a revelation as well as a visual delight.

The early history of our city comes alive in these pages, from the first days of Mission Dolores through the Gold Rush, the 1906 earthquake and fire, the development of the waterfront and the Financial District, the Panama-Pacific Exposition of 1915, and the Great Depression of the 1930s.

But *Landmarks of San Francisco* is also a contemporary story about a city's passion for preserving its heritage.

The movement that led to San Francisco's first preservation laws in the 1960s—and their continual development and strengthening over the past twenty-five years—are testimony to a citizen activism that exemplifies the caring we all feel for this special place.

Patrick McGrew and Marion Brenner have created a book that will appeal not only to architects and planners, but to anyone who has walked the streets of San Francisco and been thrilled by her beauty and vibrancy.

—ART AGNOS
Mayor

Jessie Street Substation, detail of entrance (commentary on page 136)

INTRODUCTION

While I have often espoused the point of view that one should not confuse the history of San Francisco's architecture with the history of its preservation (which is, after all, the subject of this book), I am compelled to offer the briefest possible outline of San Francisco's architectural history, if only to give the reader a simple framework upon which to evaluate what has been preserved.

Prior to the development of the missions, California architecture was literally thatched huts built by Native Americans. With the arrival of the Franciscan Fathers, construction began on a series of structures that were built from adobe bricks (Mission Dolores being the best local example). Later, craftsmen and artisans were brought from Mexico to teach the inhabitants some more complex and permanent building techniques.

Following the construction of the Mission, San Francisco, which was considered to have an inhospitable climate and poor soil, remained relatively undeveloped until the Gold Rush of 1849. The city's negative environmental aspects were compensated for by the presence of the Bay, which not only was a logical landing point for arriving passengers seeking their fortune in the gold country, but also became the best port to receive the goods required by this suddenly affluent part of America.

The earliest of these forty-niners, as they came to be called, lived in cloth tents, which were gradually insulated with paper and strengthened with wood. These became the cloth-lined cottages, some of which until fairly recently could still be found in that peculiarly isolated wooden street known as Napier Lane in the Telegraph Hill Historic District. A style that enjoyed some popularity in the district was the so-called Carpenter Gothic Style. This style is typified by the addition of a few carved redwood details of Gothic origin to the front of a typical small box of a house. While the architectural detail continued to evolve through various styles, even today San Francisco's row-house layout promotes this concept of the decorated front. The standard joke is "a Queen Anne front and a Mary Ann back!"

As the city became more settled and more permanent, prefabricated homes were imported from the East Coast, and in some ways these buildings became the model for the indigenous architecture that was to follow, even though they bore no real relationship to San Francisco's topography and climate. Both the Stanyan House and the Phelps House have their roots in this practice. More often than not, these buildings were in the Greek Revival Style. Soon, however, San Francisco's long love affair with Victorian architecture began to surface. Pattern books from the East Coast became the basis for the designs of the city's domestic buildings. Recognizing opportunity, East

Coast architects soon began to make their way to California, obviating the need for pattern books; they brought with them the fashionable European designs then popular in the major American cities.

The most recognizable of these styles are San Francisco's Victorian and Edwardian buildings. Within these categories, there exist a few variations that are often mentioned in this book. Among the Victorians are the Italianate (1860–80), which are characterized by slanted bay windows and a somewhat subdued demeanor. The Stick-Eastlake Style (1880–90) usually displays a squared bay window and is often far more elaborate than its Italianate predecessor. The last, and often most flamboyant, style is the Queen Anne (1890–1900), which is often identified by the presence of one or more round towers. The Edwardian Style represented a return to a simpler, more conservative and understated style, which saw the bay window go out of fashion.

Not only did San Francisco's residential architecture come to resemble that found on the East Coast, but so, too, did its commercial architecture. From the prototypical 1853 Montgomery Block office building (now the site of the Transamerica "pyramid") to much of Jackson Square, the city's buildings took on the look of Maine, New York, or Massachusetts. Many of the San Francisco Landmarks carry a notation making a stylistic comparison to a particular East Coast building.

By the 1890s, San Francisco's architects were being trained in Europe, so the city's buildings came more directly to resemble European styles. The best example may be the 1902 Koshland House with its façade references to Le Petit Trianon at Versailles.

Following the earthquake and fire of 1906, San Francisco was anxious to rebuild quickly. Consequently, much of what was destroyed was rebuilt in more or less the same fashion, often on existing foundations. Much of the original Victorian architecture that had existed in the fire zone was replaced with its more conservative Edwardian equivalent, but the scale and texture of the city remained remarkably unchanged.

Later, in the 1920s, a wide mixture of historical styles appeared in San Francisco, including Neo-Georgian, Mediterranean, Mission, Romanesque Revival, Tudor, and Craftsman. Most of these styles are self-explanatory, but the Craftsman Style derives from the Arts and Crafts Movement—it is later and often more responsive to the California climate. In recent times, a variation of this style has become known as the California Shingle Style. It may be characterized as having a fairly modest, all-shingled exterior, often with hooded windows and simple trims. These same ideas have proven to be remarkably durable and continue to be found in some of the newest buildings.

There was little new construction in San Francisco in the thirties. As a consequence, few Art Deco structures have received protection, although there do exist a few very fine examples. Coit Tower and Rincon Annex number among the few protected Art Deco, or Art Moderne buildings. As yet, very few contemporary buildings have been protected in San Francisco. Among them are Frank Lloyd Wright's Morris Store and Skidmore, Owings & Merrill's International Style Crown-Zellerbach Building, as well as Richard Neutra's 66 Calhoun Terrace residence, in the Telegraph Hill Historic District.

Since its inception in 1967, the San Francisco Landmarks Preservation Advisory Board has seen its work result in the designation of nearly 200 individual Landmarks and ten Historic Districts for a total of nearly 1,200 protected structures. This process also involved the review—in the form of the Certificate of Appropriateness application—of literally thousands of changes to the city's historic buildings. Nearly as much damage to architectural and historic heritage can be done through insensitive alterations (often in the name of preservation) as is done through demolition, so this review is a critical part of the process.

Nearly as important a part of the Landmarks Board's designation work is the educational role that goes with the public-hearings process. Nationally, preservation was once viewed as the domain of aging Southern ladies with too much time on their hands. Today, San Francisco's preservation community includes nearly all segments of its business, cultural, and social life, representatives of which attend hearings or are otherwise affected by the actions of the Board.

The diversity evident in this book inspires pride in what San Francisco's preservation movement has accomplished by identifying and helping to preserve the city's past. Architecturally and historically, much is represented here. Often the selection involves more than meets the eye, and there are a few structures on the roll that may no longer be worthy of the protection afforded them. The inventory of protected buildings is exactly what one might expect from a city with San Francisco's quixotic reputation.

In the early 1960s, the demolition of such well-known buildings as the old Montgomery Block or the Fox Theater began to make the citizenry wary of the future. These losses, together with the publication of *Here Today* (the first architectural survey and inventory of the city), and many years' work by concerned citizens, led to the drafting of City Planning Code, Article 10, which gave the Landmarks Board its authority. It was found that structures, sites, and areas of special character or special historical, architectural, or aesthetic interest or value were being unnecessarily destroyed or impaired, although preserving them was feasible and in the public interest.

Nearly all preservation legislation addresses the identification, protection, enhancement, and perpetuation of historic structures. In New York the contemporary preservation movement has roots in the 1800s, and many boards and commissions had been established in the United States by the 1960s and 70s. But it was not until 1978, following the Supreme Court decision in the Grand Central case, that the preservation movement was tested and legitimized. This momentous decision affirmed that cities had a right to legislate the protection of their historic resources and that landmark designation did not constitute a "taking" of property rights. Unfortunately, San Francisco's 1967 ordinance had no real teeth in it. It is a little-known fact that under this ordinance landmarks may be demolished; the law provides only for stays of demolition for a period of time (up to one year with the Board of Supervisors' concurrence) to see what alternatives might be found.

The Landmarks Board has a great track record in this regard: No officially designated landmarks have ever been demolished, although one could quibble about the façade-only retention of the 456 Montgomery project,

Landmark Numbers 109 and 110. But some buildings, such as the legendary lost City of Paris department store, never completed the designation process and therefore failed to become landmarks. Other significant losses include the Fitzhugh Building on Union Square, the Hall of Justice (the set for Raymond Burr's *Ironsides*), and the Fox Theater.

The Landmarks Board had a somewhat timid beginning. It acted originally as more of an honor society than a planning tool, and so the designations that ensued were mostly safe ones. Four of the first five recognized structures were church buildings, which at that time were not considered endangered. Churches now take a very different view of the landmarks process when they sell their land for speculative development. Today, those early designations seem more prescient than "safe"!

Some Board members could not be convinced to designate buildings if controversy was involved. Owner opposition was deemed sufficient by some to deny a designation, even when it was obvious that these same owners were responsible for the needless demolitions that were occurring. Additionally, as is often the nature of political appointments, some Board members felt they represented a certain constituency and voted more from a political sense than from any real commitment to preservation.

The Landmarks Board's honeymoon period ended soon. During 1969, most of the Board's work was focused on a few blocks of Jackson Street and Pacific Avenue near Montgomery Street. Development pressure from the adjacent Financial District saw many structures of this small prefire commercial enclave demolished to make way for parking lots.

In what was to become a continuing reactive tactic, the Board began designating individual structures in the area in such numbers that the hearing process soon was overloaded. To designate a landmark is a very cumbersome process whereby nominations need to be recommended by the Landmarks Board and then approved by the Planning Commission, the Board of Supervisors, and the Mayor. Ultimately, it became necessary to develop a comprehensive plan for protecting the Jackson Square area. With Planning Department assistance, Jackson Square became San Francisco's first Historic District in 1972.

Over the next few years, the pattern of these honor designations continued. Many Victorian houses and French-style mansions in the better neighborhoods were designated, as were more churches and public buildings. In response to political concerns about "elitism," two residences in the Hunter's Point area were added to the list. In response to downtown demolitions, Frank Lloyd Wright's Morris Store and Burnham and Root's Mills Building became landmarks, bringing the total of downtown designations to only four! While key buildings in the Financial District were being demolished to make way for new high rises, the Landmarks Board often spent its time protecting unthreatened Victorian structures.

To the Board's credit, the quality of these designations was usually high, and it should be recognized that it functioned with minimal staff assistance from the Planning Department during this period. But the question of relevance remained. Important commercial structures continued to be demolished while ardent preservationists brought research on their own Victorian residences to the Board, seeking and getting the inevitable approval. Valuable staff and hearing time was often devoted to designating the very buildings that did not immediately need landmarks protection.

Concurrently, several huge areas in San Francisco had been designated for urban renewal. These programs were administered in San Francisco by the Redevelopment Agency, which functions independently from City Planning and Building Code requirements. In fact, by 1965 the Agency's first project, the Golden Gateway Center, had already demonstrated how quickly an entire historic area (in this case the vegetable district, which had striking similarities to Jackson Square) could disappear and be replaced by a series of towers and town houses.

While unable officially to protect the many buildings in these redevelopment areas, the Landmarks Board did hammer out a series of agreements with the Agency that resulted in protecting many of the important structures in the Western Addition and the Yerba Buena Center Redevelopment Areas. While the buildings were not "listed" per se, these informal agreements continue to be helpful in resolving disputes between the two bodies.

This kind of planning helped move the Board toward a more proactive stance. Together with Heritage (the city's nonprofit preservation foundation), the Landmarks Board opted for saving many buildings by encouraging their relocation, even at the expense of site integrity. The Agency was compelled to devise plans to relocate several important buildings (now the Biedeman Place Historic District) and rehabilitate many more. The Oriental Warehouse, the Stadmuller House, and the Pacific Gas & Electric Company's Jessie Street Substation were designated during this period. They are each located in a redevelopment area.

The seventies will best be remembered in San Francisco's land-use community as a period of explosive, and many say, excessive downtown growth. The historic character and scale of the Financial District was quickly disappearing. By the late seventies, Heritage had also joined the battle to save the downtown. Recognizing that the Financial District was still largely unprotected, it financed a survey that resulted in the 1979 publication of *Splendid Survivors*, the first survey to research and evaluate every downtown building. The authors employed an evaluation system developed by Canadian preservation scholar Harold Kahlman (*The Evaluation of Historic Buildings: A Manual*), and each building was rated using quantifiable standards. Four categories—architecture, history, environment, and integrity—became the bases for rating the buildings.

The Landmarks Board soon also adopted Kahlman's standards. It used his rating system and the *Splendid Survivors* research base, and many downtown buildings began to make their way through the designation process. More than twenty-five downtown structures were nominated in 1980–82. As during the Jackson Square glut of a few years earlier, the planning staff began to see the wisdom in making a determination about each building that merited protection. The existence of the Heritage research files accelerated the designation process during this period.

A second major factor in the expedited processing of the Landmarks Board's work was the 1979 arrival in San Francisco of Jonathan Malone, then a recent graduate of the Preservation Studies Program at Boston University. Mayor Dianne Feinstein, in her reorganization of the Board, arranged for funding (initially through CETA) to provide the first full-time staffing for the Board, and Malone was hired as its secretary. With his arrival, the Board finally had an ardent and articulate full-time advocate for preservation. Sadly, Malone retired due to poor health in 1988; he died in the fall of 1990.

By this time, the Board had also recognized there was more to be gained through the designation of theme groups and Historic Districts than individual designations. Theme groups of three or four buildings at a time were nominated, as well as several Historic Districts.

Following Jackson Square were Webster Street (1981), the Northeast Waterfront (1983), Alamo Square (1984), Liberty/Hill (1985), and Telegraph Hill (1986). The Chinatown Historic District was approved in 1985 and the Civic Center Historic District, which was already a National Register District, was approved in 1988, although neither of these last two districts has completed the process and their designation has not been ratified by the Mayor.

Responding in part to this demonstrated need for historic preservation, the city Planning Director and his staff began preparation of the Downtown Plan, which, when it became law in 1985, provided designations that were much stronger than anything the Landmarks Board had done to date: It protected from demolition *in perpetuity* 249 architecturally or historically significant buildings (Category I). The plan also provided partial protection for 200 additional buildings (Categories II, III, and IV) and set up legislation for the transfer of development rights (TDRs), which allowed owners of historic properties to sell off the unused development potential above their historic properties in exchange for maintaining forever these historic buildings.

While this was seen as a major breakthrough for preservation in San Francisco, there was more to come. Following the adoption of the Downtown Plan, a citizens' initiative petition resulted in ballot Proposition M, which was passed in 1986. Not only did this proposition result in a lowering of the annual limitation for downtown construction, but Paragraphs 2 and 7, respectively, addressed neighborhood-conservation and historic-preservation issues citywide. In other words, the Landmarks Board was finally in a position to review nearly every project in San Francisco that involved the alteration or demolition of an older structure. This legislation became the last tool in the preservationists' struggle for legal recourse.

Increasingly, the Landmarks Board's role seems to be one of reviewing projects for the appropriateness of alterations. With the amount of construction still going on in San Francisco, and the limited staffing assigned to the Board (one full-time position), stronger advocacy is still only a dream. City-sponsored Neighborhood Conservation Studies have resulted in fewer demolitions. Consequently, the current Board seems to have a reduced agenda in terms of new designations. Much of its work in the last two years is reminiscent of the early years. Of its nine designations, five have been owner-initiated and for unthreatened Victorian residences. Perhaps their work is almost complete. Nearly one percent of the city's current building stock enjoys some level of protection. Additionally, private-sector work on about 14,000 Victorian structures is increasingly enlightened and sensitive. Few of these elaborate buildings are ever demolished now.

If the Board were ever to be gifted with the kind of staff enjoyed by most cities of similar size, it is likely that an overall survey would turn up some remaining buildings that might benefit from designation. One known example is the old Bethlehem Steel Shipyards, which recalls the earliest period of the Industrial Revolution. Many buildings whose physical charms are much less obvious than their historic associations could continue to be a priority for the Board. It is hard to believe that San Franciscans have allowed the demolition of such buildings as the birthplace of Alice B. Toklas, which is a State of California Point of Historic Interest! Whatever the Board's choices for the future, its work will always have a certain fascination for the urban narcissists who enjoy the retelling of their fables.

All of the information included in this book was drawn from the actual case reports in the Landmarks Board's files. In each case, I have updated or edited them, occasionally revealing my own bias. The order in which they were designated is indicated by the Landmark Number, and they are published here roughly in that sequence. When known, the original name is given first, followed by the common or current name in parentheses. Any erroneous information is the responsibility of this writer.

MISSION
SAN FRANCISCO
DE ASIS

(Mission Dolores)

320 Dolores Street

Mission San Francisco de Asis (Mission Dolores), the oldest essentially unaltered structure in San Francisco, was built between 1782 and 1791 by Native Americans under the direction of Franciscan Father Francisco Palou. It takes its name from a nearby pond or creek, "Dolores," now gone. In the adjoining cemetery are buried many well-known early residents, including Don Luis Antonio Arguello, the first governor of California under Mexican rule. The church was restored in 1916 under the direction of the architect Willis Polk, and a steel frame was inserted into the walls to reinforce the original structure. Mission Dolores was the sixth of the chain of Spanish missions to be established along the California coast and is considered the most intact in terms of its original materials and furnishings. People who are given a "Key to the City" are told that it is a replica of the key to the Mission and that it will actually unlock its doors. *Landmark Number 1*

OLD ST. MARY'S CHURCH

660 California Street

Old St. Mary's Church was erected in 1853–54. A brick Victorian Gothic Style church, it was the original Catholic cathedral in San Francisco. The church was gutted by fire following the 1906 earthquake and was subsequently rebuilt. Its granite foundations were cut to order in China, and its bricks came from New England. The original design included a 200-foot-tall spire, which was never built. Old St. Mary's remained the Catholic cathedral until New St. Mary's was built on Van Ness Avenue in 1893. On May 6, 1966, Old St. Mary's was designated as California Registered Historical Landmark Number 810. *Landmark Number 2*

BANK OF CALIFORNIA

400 California Street

The Bank of California is the oldest incorporated commercial bank in the state. It was founded in 1864 by Darius Ogden Mills and William Chapman Ralston, who was often referred to as "the man who built San Francisco." The bank helped finance the Southern Pacific Steamship Lines and the Comstock Mines in Nevada. It is the only federally chartered national bank operating in all of the Pacific Coast states. Its original head office, built in 1867, occupied this site. Just before the fire in 1906 it was demolished to make way for the present structure. This building, by architects Bliss and Faville, was modeled after the Bank of the Knickerbocker Trust Company on Fifth Avenue in New York, which was designed by McKim, Mead & White. The Bank of California has chosen to integrate this historic banking hall into its adjacent high-rise headquarters building (1965), utilizing the air rights of the historic site. *Landmark Number 3*

St. Patrick's Church
784 Mission Street

This is the patronal church of the Irish in San Francisco. Its cornerstone was laid in 1869 and construction was completed in 1872. Built of brick in the Gothic Revival Style that dominated the era, the church was the second in the parish and replaced an earlier wooden one that had been located on Market between Second and Third streets. The wooden church has been moved to 1820 Eddy Street (see Landmark No. 6). This parish was important when neighboring Rincon Hill was still a fashionable residential neigh-borhood. Consequently, St. Patrick's Church represents an era and a residential area of the city that have vanished.

During the 1906 earthquake and fire, the interior of St. Patrick's was destroyed, leaving only the exterior walls and the tower. It was completely rebuilt except for the original steeple, which had reached 200 feet above the street. Today, St. Patrick's and St. Mary's serve the daily spiritual needs of Catholic faithful in the business district. *Landmark Number 4*

St. Francis of Assisi Church

610 Vallejo Street

The first Roman Catholic parish in San Francisco, St. Francis Parish was founded in 1849 to save the residents of the village of Yerba Buena (later San Francisco) from making the long, dusty, seven-mile trip to Mission Dolores. Construction of the present building commenced in 1857 (date of cornerstone) and was completed in 1860. The church was dedicated by Archbishop Alemany; it originally offered Mass in English, Spanish, and French.

After the fire of 1906 gutted the interior, it was restored between 1907 and 1913 and rededicated in 1918. Alemany performed the first northern California ordination of priests in this building. *Landmark Number 5*

OLD ST. PATRICK'S CHURCH
1820 Eddy Street

The oldest frame church building standing in San Francisco, Old St. Patrick's was originally constructed in 1854 on the south side of Market at the corner of Annie Street on a portion of the site now occupied by the Palace Hotel. Following the construction of the current St. Patrick's, this building was moved (in 1873) to its second site on Eddy near Laguna Street where it served the Parish of St. John the Baptist. In 1891 it was moved to its current location in Holy Cross Parish. It is now the parish hall for the new church built on an adjacent site. This building has served three parishes and also was Pro-Cathedral from 1885 to 1891 while St. Mary's at O'Farrell Street and Van Ness Avenue was being constructed. *Landmark Number 6*

AUDIFFRED BUILDING
1 Mission Street

This building was erected in 1889 by Frenchman Hippolite d'Audiffret (anglicized later to Audiffred). He built in the style of late-nineteenth-century France to remind himself of his homeland. It is one of the few structures in the vicinity to escape destruction in 1906. The building existed for nearly ninety years with much of its ground floor devoted to its original use as a saloon, once the Bulkhead, later the Silver Dollar. The upper floors had a variety of uses, ranging from rooms for sailors to studios for artists and musicians, an art school, offices for various seamen's associations, and finally a rescue mission.

The building was completely restored (and a new top floor added in 1983) and now serves as offices for attorneys. It is listed on the National Register of Historic Places. *Landmark Number 7*

SOUTH SAN FRANCISCO OPERA HOUSE

1601 Newcomb Avenue

The name of this structure bears two pieces of misinformation: it is not located in South San Francisco and it is not an opera house. Built in 1888 by the Masons, it was given an "operatic" name, as was the custom for many theaters built in America during that period, even though opera was never performed here. A more typical entertainment was the Medicine Show of Pawnee Bill. This building is said to contain the only remaining prefire theater in San Francisco. *Landmark Number 8*

LANGERMAN'S BUILDING
(Belli Building)
722 Montgomery Street

GANELLA BUILDING
(Belli Annex)
728–730 Montgomery Street

The first structure on this site was built in 1849 as a warehouse; it was destroyed by a fire in 1851. The current structure was rebuilt upon the foundations of its predecessor. For a time, this building housed the Melodeon Theater, where Lotta Crabtree performed. Through the years the building has housed many different occupants, none as well known as its current occupant, attorney Melvin Belli, who purchased the building in 1959 and converted it into law offices. The structure is built upon 8-inch-thick wooden planks laid to a depth of 8 feet. This wooden foundation was laid directly into the mud of what was then an inlet of San Francisco Bay; it is said that the tide still rises and falls in the elevator shaft. *Landmark Number 9*

Records indicate that this structure was built by Joseph Ganella for his china business as well as his residence. The building has served many other businesses over time, including gold-bullion dealers, merchandise brokers, *La Voz de Chile* (a Spanish-language newspaper), and mining company offices. A plaque on the building certifies that the first Masonic Lodge meeting in San Francisco was held on this site in 1849. Here, too, in the 1850s, Bret Harte wrote *The Luck of Roaring Camp.* As early as 1854, the upper floor was used as a meeting hall for the Odd Fellows, and later by the ancient Jewish order KBS and the American Protestant Association. In the 1880s the third floor became known as Xenon's Hall. Later it became a bathhouse, a puppet theater, a garment factory; now it contains law offices. *Landmark Number 10*

HOTALING STABLES BUILDING

32–42 Hotaling Place

(Not Pictured) This was originally constructed in the 1860s as two buildings, one a stable for the other, which housed a brokerage firm: W. Pierce & Company. These buildings were connected at one time by a tunnel beneath Hotaling Place (originally Jones Alley) to Pierce's main office on Montgomery Street. *Landmark Number 11*

HOTALING BUILDING

451 Jackson Street

Built in 1866, this is a well-known survivor of the great earthquake and fire of 1906. The building was the headquarters and warehouse of the extensive liquor, real-estate, and trading company of A. P. Hotaling & Sons. For over fifty years it was a bonded-liquor warehouse and was used in conjunction with other liquor-warehousing buildings in the district. The building also housed the highly regarded collection of books and paintings amassed by Hotaling, who was considered a connoisseur. It was restored in 1951. *Landmark Number 12*

HOTALING ANNEX EAST

445 Jackson Street

The Hotaling Annex East, at 445 Jackson Street, was built in 1860. Its first owner is unknown. It is known that in 1871 the building was occupied by the Tremont Stables, which served the Tremont Hotel at 420 Jackson Street until 1870. The building was later purchased and occupied by A. P. Hotaling as part of his liquor business. It is likely that he altered it at that time to reflect the design of his original building at 451 Jackson. It was renovated in 1951. *Landmark Number 13*

Medico-Dental Building

441 Jackson Street

This building was constructed in 1861 atop the hulls of two ships abandoned during the Gold Rush. Over time, it housed various tenants typical of the area, including wine-and-liquor importers and coffee mills. Like much of Jackson Square, it was restored in the early 1950s as showrooms for the wholesale-furnishings industry. *Landmark Number 14*

GHIRARDELLI BUILDING

415-431 Jackson Street

This building is said to have been constructed in 1853 as offices for Domingo Ghirardelli and Company, the chocolate manufacturers. In 1869 the building was also occupied by the Buena Vista Vinacultural Society, wine makers and dealers, whose officers included Joseph Donohoe, John Parrott, and William Ralston. Also housed here was the Italian weekly newspaper *Eco della Patria*. The Ghirardelli Factory moved in 1900, but the offices and retail shop remained until 1904. The building then became a woodworking mill and finishing shop. By the 1920s, it had become a cigar factory; in the forties it housed a printshop, and in the fifties it became a furniture showroom. *Landmark Number 15*

GHIRARDELLI BUILDING ANNEX

407 Jackson Street

The age of this building is not certain, but it was probably built in 1861. In 1873 it was occupied by James W. Wheeler & Company, a firm of carriage painters. At some later date, possibly around 1880, it was purchased by the Ghirardelli Company, and its use then closely paralleled that of its neighbor at 415 Jackson Street (Landmark No. 15). *Landmark Number 16*

McElroy Octagon House

(Colonial Dames Octagon House-Museum)
2645 Gough Street

One of two remaining octagonal houses in San Francisco, this one was built in 1861 by William C. McElroy. Octagonal houses throughout the United States owe their origin and vogue during the 1850s and 60s to the publication of *A Home for All* in 1848 by New Yorker Orson Squire Fowler, a book intended to stimulate the building of American houses based upon a new and more rational (octagonal) plan. Designed to provide eight rooms on each of two floors, this plan was advocated as most healthful because it gave each room maximum sunlight. It is thought that as many as five octagonal houses were built in San Francisco.

The building has lost its site integrity: it was relocated from its original lot across Union Street in the 1950s. A 1906 Arnold Genthe photograph shows the damage the building sustained during the earthquake. *Landmark Number 17*

PALACE HOTEL
(Sheraton Palace Hotel)
Market at New Montgomery Street

The postfire Palace Hotel was designed by East Coast architect George Kelham. He was sent to San Francisco by the firm of Trowbridge and Livingston in 1907 to supervise the construction of the new Palace Hotel, the original having been destroyed in 1906. He remained in San Francisco and later received such prestigious commissions as the Public Library in the Civic Center. In the new Palace Hotel, he designed a great interior space, the Garden Court, which is reminiscent of the original carriage entrance but rises only to the third floor. This space became the city's banquet hall. It is used for occasions requiring the seating of nearly one thousand people. It has also been the hotel's dining room, theater, ballroom, and concert hall. For many years, the San Francisco Symphony played concerts here. The building was completely renovated in 1990. *Landmark Number 18*

HOTALING ANNEX WEST

463–473 Jackson Street

Built in the Italianate Style of the 1860s and contemporary with other buildings on this block of Jackson Street, 463 Jackson closely resembles the Hotaling offices and warehouse on the opposite corner of Hotaling Place. However, prior to Hotaling, this building was occupied by Dominic Small, who maintained a carpentry shop here. The building was purchased by Hotaling in the late 1880s to expand his liquor-wholesaling business. *Landmark Number 20*

GOLDEN ERA BUILDING

732 Montgomery Street

Built in 1852 upon foundations of an earlier building destroyed in the fire of 1851, this building housed an early newspaper, *The Golden Era*. Bret Harte worked as a typesetter and authored his first poem here, which was published in 1857. During the 1860s the building was used as an appliance store, a crockery shop, and a billiard-table factory. Later, the upper floor was converted into a meeting hall for the Lafayette Guard, a militia company. Following the rejuvenation of Jackson Square in the 1950s as the wholesale furnishings district, this building housed the showroom and offices of Knoll International, which specializes in architect-designed furnishings. *Landmark Number 19*

SAN FRANCISCO CITY HALL

100 Polk Street

Constructed in 1913–15, during an era of architectural magnificence, City Hall, like most public buildings of the period, is in the Classical Style. Architects Bakewell and Brown, who studied architecture in Paris at the Ecole des Beaux-Arts, designed this building, which is generally considered to be one of the finest examples of French Renaissance Revival architecture in the country. Monumental in concept and design, City Hall is a rectangle 400 feet long and 300 feet deep. It is capped with a central dome that divides the interior into two light courts. The rotunda, rising through all four principal floors of the building to the underside of the dome, is the chief interior feature of the building. *Landmark Number 21*

LARCO'S BUILDING
(Solari Building East)
470 Jackson Street

OLD FRENCH CONSULATE
(Solari Building West)
472 Jackson Street

This building was constructed around 1852 by Nicholas Larco, prominent merchant and leader of San Francisco's Italian colony. Larco dealt in liquor and dry goods, in addition to being a commission merchant, and he occupied the building until 1877. Larco's Building has housed the consulates of three nations. In 1856 Larco himself was consul for Chile; one of his tenants here was Camillo Martin, who was the consul for Spain. From 1861 to 1865 France's consul, Charles de Gazotte, had his consulate here. *Landmark Number 22*

Built in 1850 and originally occupied by the French-wine-and-liquor firm of C. Lagauterie and Company, 472 Jackson is considered the oldest building in Jackson Square. In 1865, the French consul, Charles de Gazotte, relocated the consulate here, where it remained until 1876 (although de Gazotte died of smallpox in 1868). *Landmark Number 23*

Tremont Hotel Building

(Yeon Building)

423 Jackson Street

Research in Jackson Square has resulted in thorough histories of most of its buildings, with this one exception; little is known about 432 Jackson. Conflicting stories indicate it may have been the Tremont Hotel and that it may, at one time, have housed the French Consulate. It is safe to say that it is one of the most beautiful buildings in Jackson Square. *Landmark Number 24*

MOULANIE BUILDING

448-460 Jackson Street

This lot was acquired by a French sea captain during the Gold Rush and has been owned until very recently by his descendants, who have always resided in France. The building was constructed in the 1850s as an investment property, and its first known occupant was C. Lagauterie, who relocated from 472 Jackson. Tenants after 1900 included a tannery, a seed company, and an interior-design firm. *Landmark Number 25*

BANK OF LUCAS, TURNER & COMPANY

800–804 Montgomery Street

This bank was built in 1853 by Keyser and Brown after designs by architect Reuben Clark; its construction was supervised by William Tecumseh Sherman, who was later to become famous as a Civil War general.

Originally three stories tall, with its more elaborately detailed façade facing Montgomery Street, this structure is recorded as having cost $53,000, a large sum for the day. The top floor was damaged and subsequently removed during the 1906 earthquake and fire. The Bank of Lucas, Turner & Company moved in during the summer of 1854 and remained until their voluntary liquidation in 1857. *Landmark Number 26*

GROGAN-LENT-ATHERTON BUILDING

400 Jackson Street

A building erected on this site in 1858 housed the real-estate business of Alexander B. Grogan and his financier-partner William M. Lent. The identity of the prefire building as this structure has not been completely established. In 1906 the building was severely damaged by the earthquake. A photograph from the *San Francisco Examiner* depicts this as the first brick building completed after the fire. It is not clear whether it is completely new or the reconstruction of an existing building. Photographic documentation of similarities between the two structures is insufficient to establish conclusively that these are, in fact, the same building. *Landmark Number 27*

St. Stephen's
Episcopal Church

(Old Holy Virgin Russian Orthodox Church)

858–864 Fulton Street

This German-Renaissance Style church was constructed in 1880 and remained an Episcopal church until it was sold to a Russian Orthodox congregation in 1930. It then became the principal cathedral of the International Russian Orthodox Church until 1961, when a modern structure was built in the Outer Richmond District. It continues to serve the Russian community in the neighborhood. *Landmark Number 28*

Firehouse,
Engine Company No. 22

(Oakes Children's Center)

1348 Tenth Avenue

(Not Pictured) Constructed in 1898, this was the first firehouse built in the then-developing Sunset District. It housed Engine Company No. 22 for sixty-four years. The men of this company played an important role in the events of April 1906. Along with the men of Company No. 30, they assisted in the evacuation of patients from Park Emergency Hospital. For forty-five hours, the company patrolled the streets as far east as Hyde and as far north as Sacramento Street, lending assistance as required.

In 1962, Engine Company No. 22 moved to new quarters. The old structure was declared surplus and sold at auction. Although it has suffered substantial and unsympathetic alterations, the firehouse continues to serve the community, now as a center for emotionally disturbed children. *Landmark Number 29*

PIONEER WOOLEN MILL AND D. GHIRARDELLI COMPANY

(Ghirardelli Square)
North Point at Larkin
Street

The buildings located on this block are among the most historic in San Francisco. They were constructed over a period of more than a century, beginning with the Pioneer Woolen Mill (1859), which manufactured uniforms for the Union Army during the Civil War. Subsequent buildings constructed by the Ghirardelli interests include the Mustard Building, the Chocolate Factory, and most important, the Clocktower (1915), inspired by the tower of the Château de Blois in France. The entire complex was considered so historically and architecturally important to San Francisco that William Matson Roth, who owned it in the 1950s, commissioned architects Wurster, Bernardi and Emmons, together with landscape architect Lawrence Halprin, to develop a scheme for the adaptive reuse of the buildings. This project, Ghirardelli Square, became one of the earliest and best examples of this type of conversion and continues to be a model for similar conversions throughout the United States. *Landmark Number 30*

Burr House
1772 Vallejo Street

Ephraim William Burr, one-time mayor of San Francisco, commissioned this mansion as a wedding present for his son Edmond and Edmond's bride, Anna Barnard, in 1875. The construction of the building was supervised by Miss Barnard's father, Thomas, to the designs of Edmund M. Wharff. Although primarily Italianate, the building also exhibits influences of the then-emerging Second Empire Style of French architecture, most notably its mansard roof. One of the best-preserved and handsomest of its style and period, it is viewed as a transitional building architecturally because of its more modern, eclectic design. *Landmark Number 31*

PHELPS HOUSE
1111 Oak Street

Although accounts vary as to its dates and builder, the Abner Phelps House is generally considered to be the oldest extant residence in San Francisco. The earliest published account suggests the structure was built in 1850 by John Middleton and Sons, one of the first real-estate concerns in the city. It was said to be constructed from lumber framed into sections in Maine and brought around Cape Horn for assembly, there being no sawmills in San Francisco at that time. In a later oral history, Phelps's great-granddaughter indicated the house was purchased in New Orleans, shipped here in sections, and reassembled to appease the homesickness of her great-grandmother Augusta. Later research, however, revealed that the house is, in fact, constructed of California redwood. It is known that the house has been moved three times. The first move coincided with the grading and construction of Divisadero Street in the 1890s. In 1904, the structure was moved to the back of the lot to allow for the construction of commercial properties on Divisadero Street. The last move saw the house turned 180 degrees to form the centerpiece of a historic compound that includes another landmark structure. *Landmark Number 32*

SENTINEL BUILDING

916 Kearny Street

One of the city's earliest "skyscrapers," the Sentinel Building was constructed at the gore corner of Columbus Avenue and Kearny Street and marks the confluence of downtown, Chinatown, Jackson Square, and North Beach. Designed by architects Salfield and Kohlberg, this structurally advanced building was under construction during the 1906 earthquake and suffered no damage. No expense was spared by those responsible for its building, the most notable of whom was Abraham "Boss" Reuf. Reuf had intended to locate his offices here, advantageously situated near the old City Hall. However, the graft prosecutions of 1907 interrupted his project, and it was not until his release from San Quentin in 1915 that he was able to realize his plans. After a period of decline in the 1940s and 50s, the building was restored in 1958 and continues in office use today. Academy Award-winning filmmaker Francis Ford Coppola, who owns the building, maintains offices here. *Landmark Number 33*

UNITED STATES MINT AND SUBTREASURY

608 Commercial Street

In 1852, a building on this site was purchased by the Federal government from a private assaying company. After alterations, it was opened as a branch mint in 1854. In the early days, the Mint had two purposes. The first was to coin money and the second was to store coined gold and silver while serving unofficially as an early type of Federal Reserve Bank. In 1875, the original structure was demolished and a new four-story building was constructed atop the original foundations and vaults. The minting functions had been moved to a new building at Fifth and Mission streets a year earlier, so this new building served only as a subtreasury. In 1906, the building was badly damaged and subsequently reduced to the one-story structure visible today. In 1915, the treasury was relocated to its own building at Sansome and Pine streets. The original building continued to house government offices until 1922, when it was sold to private interests. In the mid-eighties, the building was converted to a private museum of the Pacific by its owner, the Bank of Canton, who also built its high-rise headquarters on an adjacent lot. *Landmark Number 34*

STADMULLER HOUSE

819 Eddy Street

(Not Pictured) Designed by architect P. R. Schmidt, this residence was constructed in 1880 for Frederick D. Stadmuller, who came to San Francisco in 1879 from Silver City, Nevada, where he had owned a chain of mercantile stores (Stadmuller & Company) and a timber concern. After his relocation, he became associated with the firm of Walter, Schilling & Company, dealers in California wines and brandies. The house remained in the Stadmuller family until 1951 when it was sold to new owners who converted the building into a rooming house. This use was discontinued when it was sold again and converted back to a single-family residence in 1963. The interior of the house has been carefully restored in the Victorian style with authentic colors, wall coverings, lighting, and draperies. *Landmark Number 35*

KENNY OCTAGON HOUSE

(Feusier Octagon House)

1067 Green Street

The circa-1852 Kenny House is the older and more elegant of the two remaining octagonal houses built in San Francisco. George L. Kenny was its first known owner. However, the building is commonly associated with the name Feusier, in whose family it was to remain for some eighty years. The house appears in early photographs of the city, including one dated 1858. Standing alone near the summit of Russian Hill, it was a familiar landmark of the time.

The original two-story house was modified late in the nineteenth century by the Feusiers, when they added the mansard-roofed third floor surmounted by an octagonal cupola. As was the case with many Russian Hill structures, this building survived the earthquake. It was, however, menaced by the ensuing fire, which caused the outbuildings to be dynamited as a fire stop to save the main house. *Landmark Number 36*

HALLIDIE BUILDING

130 Sutter Street

Named for cable car inventor Andrew S. Hallidie, this steel-framed, glass-curtain-walled building designed by Willis Polk and completed in 1918 is the world's first curtain-walled building and one of the best of its kind anywhere. Although its front façade is lightly ornamented with Gothic-style cast-iron tracery, it may still be viewed as the earliest and one of the most innovative modern structures in the country. *Landmark Number 37*

BOURNE MANSION

2550 Webster Street

The Bourne Mansion was designed by famed San Francisco architect Willis Polk for civic leader and philanthropist William B. Bourne, who headed the Spring Valley Water Company, Pacific Gas & Electric, and Grass Valley's Empire Mining Company. Bourne helped finance the 1915 Panama-Pacific Exposition and is considered the last "empire builder" of the West. The restrained dark-brick exterior of the building, with few openings, gives way to an elaborate interior that features a monumental staircase with high-polished bannisters leading to an imposing ballroom across the entire front of the house at the second level. This town house was the first residence Polk designed for Bourne, the other being the historic Filoli, the country home that was used in the television series *Dynasty. Landmark Number 38*

ST. ANSGAR DANISH LUTHERAN CHURCH
(St. Francis Lutheran Church)
152 Church Street

This charming red-brick neighborhood church was built in 1905, with financial assistance from Queen Louise of Denmark, as a religious center for Danish immigrants in San Francisco. During the 1906 earthquake and fire, the still-unfinished structure was used by the Red Cross as a hospital and shelter for the injured and the homeless. In 1965 the congregation merged with the Finnish Gethsemane Lutheran Church and adopted its present name. *Landmark Number 39*

First Unitarian Church

Franklin at Geary Street

The first Unitarian services in San Francisco were held in 1850. Though now occupying its third building, the current congregation traces its roots directly to those first services. Prominent Unitarians historically associated with those original services include Thomas Starr King, who ministered to the congregation for four years (1860–64); Captain Frederick Macondray; James Otis, mayor of San Francisco (1873–75); jeweler George Shreve; Leland Stanford; Bret Harte; Andrew Hallidie; and Ralph Waldo Emerson.

The present church, designed by George W. Percy, was built in 1887–89. It remains largely unchanged except that a bell tower and steeple destroyed in 1906 were replaced with a square turret, built along original lines. Congregation members associated with the current building include Julia Ward Howe, author of "The Battle Hymn of the Republic"; Edward Everett Hale, the orator; and a former president of Harvard University. A recent addition to the church, designed by Charles Warren Callister, was dedicated in 1968. *Landmark Number 40*

St. Mark's Evangelical Lutheran Church

1135 O'Farrell Street

Descending directly from the earliest Lutheran congregations in California at the time of the Gold Rush, St. Mark's was built in 1895 from designs by the prominent architect Henry Geilfuss. The building survived the 1906 disaster with little damage, due primarily to the dynamiting along Van Ness Avenue, which served as a barrier to the encroaching fire. As was the case with most public and religious buildings, St. Mark's was also pressed into service as a refuge for many of the injured, homeless, and bereaved. St. Mark's is a red-brick church in the Romanesque Revival Style with some minor Gothic ornamentation. Solid and heavy, it embodies a massiveness and scale uncommon in California religious architecture. *Landmark Number 41*

SULLIVAN MEMORIAL FIRE CHIEF'S RESIDENCE
870 Bush Street

This building owes its existence to the death of San Francisco Fire Chief Dennis T. Sullivan in 1906. Sullivan resided on the third floor of the engine house near Bush and Kearny streets, literally in the shadow of the California Hotel and Theater. When the earthquake struck on the morning of April 18, parts of the hotel parapet fell through the roof of the engine house, fatally wounding Chief Sullivan. The fire department was thus leaderless in its hours of greatest trial, another sensational detail of the horror of the day.

The chief's residence was built in 1921 as a memorial to Sullivan, and it remains one of the smallest and most gracious downtown structures. San Francisco is one of the few cities that still provides a residence for the chief of its fire department. *Landmark Number 42*

CABLE CAR BARN AND POWERHOUSE
Northwest corner of Washington and Mason Streets

This is the only surviving cable car barn and powerhouse in the city, some fourteen of which at one time or another served the various cable-car lines. Although cable propulsion was invented in England early in the nineteenth century, its successful operation did not occur until Andrew S. Hallidie's cable car made its inaugural run up the Clay Street hill, beginning at Portsmouth Plaza, on August 1, 1873. The world-wide interest generated by San Francisco's success lasted well into the 1890s, when the advent of electric railways eclipsed the cable cars. In the 1880s, when cable-car systems were at the height of their popularity, they existed in a score of cities, including Edinburgh, Melbourne, Brooklyn, and Constantinople. San Francisco was then, and fortunately has remained, the world's cable-car capital and its cable cars are National Historic Monuments—the only ones that move! The original three-story building, dating from 1885, was largely destroyed in 1906. It was reconstructed to a generally similar appearance, although only two stories in height. *Landmark Number 43*

Presbyterian Mission House

(Donaldina Cameron House) 920 Sacramento Street

The fame of this building is connected with Donaldina Cameron who was born in New Zealand in 1869, but lived in California from 1871. Cameron headed the Mission House and resided in it for more than forty years. The building served as a shelter for young Chinese women who were rescued from a thriving slave trade in the latter 1800s. They were given refuge here until arrangements were made for rehabilitation, emigration, or marriage. As many as fifty young women could be accommodated by the shelter. Additionally, de-serted or orphaned Chinese children benefited from the charitable activities of the devoted women who staffed this mission under the auspices of the Presbyterian Church. The mission was responsible for the establishment in California of many other Chinese homes and orphanages where young women were trained in domestic arts. Built in 1881, and rebuilt in 1907 on the original foundations but in a different style, the building was officially dedicated in honor of Donaldina Cameron on June 7, 1942. *Landmark Number 44*

LEALE HOUSE
2575 Pacific Avenue

This small but elegant house, which dates from the 1850s, was
originally a four-room structure situated on what was then a 25-acre
dairy farm operated by Joel Clayton. Its name comes from its best-
known occupant, ferryboat captain John Leale, who resided here
from 1886. Captain Leale's fame derives from his autobiography,
Recollections of a Tule Sailor. The one-story structure, finished with
rustic siding, features a false high front in the Italianate manner.
The present front porch was added later, as was the Italianate Style
garage, built in 1980. *Landmark Number 45*

SHEPPARD-DAKIN HOUSE

(House of the Flag) 1652–1656 Taylor Street

According to local legend, the House of the Flag survived the 1906 earthquake because its occupant, a flag collector, raised a flag atop the building before abandoning it to the oncoming fire; he felt the building should go down with "all flags flying." This effort so inspired a group of fire fighters that they put forth the extra effort necessary to save the house. Built in two parts, the lower in 1860 and the upper in 1903, the building is considered a minor example of the California Shingle Style, once very commonplace and now increasingly rare on Russian Hill. *Landmark Number 46*

NIGHTINGALE HOUSE
201 Buchanan Street

This house was built by John Nightingale as his own residence. Nightingale was a real estate dealer responsible for the construction of many of the Victorian houses in the neighborhood. He was a forty-niner who became an early San Francisco Alderman, president of the Society of California Pioneers, and later, one of the trustees of the massive James Lick Estate. He was involved in the site selection of the 1870 City Hall, which was destroyed by the earthquake in 1906.

Although the architect of Nightingale house is unknown, it is considered a masterpiece of the Eastlake Style and is one of the very rare examples of the rural type of Victorian house (horizontal rather than vertical) remaining in San Francisco. It incorporates elements of the Carpenter Gothic, Second Empire, and Italian Villa styles. *Landmark Number 47*

SHERMAN HOUSE

(Sherman House Hotel)

2160 Green Street

Built in 1876, this spacious Victorian residence was designed for Leander S. Sherman, founder of one of the nation's oldest and largest music stores, Sherman, Clay & Company. Sherman was an early and important patron of both the symphony and the opera.

The entire west wing houses a music room, which is three stories high and skylighted. It originally contained a platform for musicians, as well as a balcony from which many of the world's leading musical figures performed, including Lotta Crabtree and Ignace Paderewski.

Primarily Italianate in design, the Sherman House also gives evidence of French Second Empire influences, particularly in its mansard roof. It is one of the handsomest and best-preserved Victorian structures in San Francisco.

When the building was designated in 1972, it was owned by sculptor Beatrice Herbert, who used the music room as studio space. After her death, the building was converted to a small, elegant hotel. *Landmark Number 49*

DIETLE HOUSE

294 Page Street

(Not Pictured) This house was designed and built by well-known San Francisco architect Henry Geilfuss for Charles Dietle, a prize bootmaker. In 1906 it was sold to John DeMartini, who was one of the original directors of the Bank of Italy. Tall and spacious with a strong vertical thrust, the house has two stories over a basement and covers nearly all of its site. The quality of this finely detailed Stick Style building is shown in its squared bays; vertical strip elements; ornate carvings on the bays, porch, and gables; and eave brackets. Original wrought-iron railings still separate the small front garden from the sidewalk. *Landmark Number 48*

CASEBOLT HOUSE
2727 Pierce Street

Henry Casebolt was a wealthy pioneer carriage builder. He built this impressive three-story wood-frame residence around 1865 on a hill not far from his carriage factory in Cow Hollow. The house is considered a masterpiece of Italianate Style. Its most prominent feature is the centrally located porch, flanked by double stairways. Corinthian columns support the foremost section of the porch and are reflected in matching pilasters that flank the front door. The columns and pilasters give rise to the entablature of the porch, which is surmounted by a balcony and topped by a broken pediment at the roof.

It was this house that graced the cover of the popular book *Here Today,* some twenty years ago. *Here Today* is credited with influencing the formation of the Landmarks Board, as well as the city's nonprofit Foundation for San Francisco's Architectural Heritage. *Landmark Number 51*

THE CONSERVATORY

John F. Kennedy Drive
Golden Gate Park

This exquisitely anachronistic Victorian conservatory, modeled after the Conservatory in the Royal Botanical Gardens of Kew, England, was constructed in 1878. It is one of the largest such buildings in the United States, covering 15,000 square feet. It was the first municipal greenhouse in California, as well as the first structure to be erected in Golden Gate Park, and it is considered by many to be the most beautiful. It was built by greenhouse manufacturers Lord and Burnham of Irvington, New York at the direction of San Francisco magnate James Lick. It is made of components that were hauled from the East Coast in a ship especially chartered for that purpose. The Conservatory in Golden Gate Park is listed on the National Register and is California Registered Historical Landmark No. 841. *Landmark Number 50*

BANCO POPULARE ITALIANO OPERAIA FUGAZI

(Old Transamerica Building)

4 Columbus Avenue

This building was constructed in 1909 for the Banco Populare Italiano Operaia Fugazi, founded by John F. Fugazi immediately after the 1906 disaster. The Fugazi continued to operate for some years as an independent bank. Ultimately it was acquired by the Bank of Italy, which later became the Bank of America. The Fugazi emerged from this banking empire in 1938 as the Transamerica Corporation and became independent of the Bank of America in the 1950s.

The original design by Charles Paff showed a five-story building. However, the building originally constructed was two stories high with a small ornate cupola. Before 1914, the building was enlarged vertically with the addition of a third floor. In recent years the building was lengthened horizontally to the appearance it retains today. *Landmark Number 52*

WORMSER-COLEMAN HOUSE

1834 California Street

This house was constructed in 1876 for Isaac Wormser, a pioneer San Francisco merchant. Wormser resided in the house until 1895, when it was sold to John C. Coleman, a successful gold miner. Coleman remodeled the house to accommodate his large family and added to the original site by purchasing a 50-foot-wide piece of land to the west and adding it to the original lot. It was used for open space and gardens.

This two-story wood-frame Italianate structure is considered one of the most graceful homes in San Francisco. Together with the other late-nineteenth and early-twentieth-century houses on the block, it makes an enclave of architecturally significant structures that represent a fashionable neighborhood from an earlier San Francisco era. *Landmark Number 53*

COLEMAN HOUSE

1701 Franklin Street

This house was designed by architects Salfield and Kohlberg and built for Edward Coleman, a successful gold miner and brother of John Coleman (see Landmark No. 53). This three-story, wood-frame building is celebrated for its definitive Queen Anne styling. With three principal façades, the house has an air of solidity and massiveness. The north façade (pictured) gives exterior expression to the interior grand stair. The façade facing California Street is more balanced than the one facing Franklin Street. The basic elements of the California Street façade are the rusticated brown-stone basement, bay windows on each of the principal floors, and towers at each corner of the attic story. These elements produce an impression of imposing grandeur. Two prominent features of this façade are the hexagonal uphill tower on the west and the round downhill tower on the east. Each is capped with a conical roof.
Landmark Number 54

LILIENTHAL-PRATT HOUSE
1818-1824 California Street

This house was built in 1876 by Louis Sloss as a wedding present for his daughter Estelle and her husband, Ernest L. Lilienthal. In 1907, the Lilienthals sold the house to Orville C. Pratt, Jr., a former president of the San Francisco Bar Association and a distinguished attorney. The two-story frame house is a definitive demonstration of Victorian architecture. The impressive front façade reflects basic Italianate lines with complementary elements of the Stick Style. The corners of the house are trimmed with quoins, rendering a finished look to the exterior. The ship lap-timbers covering the side walls create a striking contrast to the elaborate front façade. The entrance porch on the west of the front façade balances the two-story angular bay window on the east. Partially fluted Corinthian columns and square pilasters support the projecting porch roof. *Landmark Number 55*

ROOS HOUSE
3500 Jackson Street

In 1909, Leon L. Roos commissioned the brilliant and innovative California architect Bernard Maybeck to build the two-story English stucco and half-timber house while he and his wife were on their honeymoon in Europe. Described as Maybeck's most urbane residence, the wood-frame structure is an adaptation of English half-timber style combined with typical Maybeck Gothic influences. The house is located at the northwest corner of Jackson and Locust streets, and its romantic appeal is heightened by the pastoral setting provided by the adjacent grounds of the Presidio, a historic fort. Recently restored, the Roos house remains in the hands of descendants of the original owners. *Landmark Number 56*

TALBOT-DUTTON HOUSE
1782 Pacific Avenue

Original records indicate water service for this structure was requested by William C. Talbot, a wealthy lumberman, in May 1875. The house was built as a gift for Talbot's daughter Mary and her husband, Henry Dutton, Jr. After serving many subsequent owners, the house was in a state of decline when it was purchased and restored in 1957. The building is considered to be an excellent example of an Italianate town house. *Landmark Number 57*

SAN FRANCISCO GAS LIGHT COMPANY

3640 Buchanan Street

In 1884, under the direction of Joseph B. Crockett, the San Francisco Gas Light Company purchased three blocks bounded by Webster, Laguna, and Bay streets, and the Bay itself. In 1891 construction began on the predominantly brick buildings that would become the new gasworks. Upon its completion in 1893, the complex was hailed as the most modern and best designed in the United States, an acknowledgment of Crockett, to whom its design and architecture are attributed. The handsomely landscaped and spacious areas between the buildings in the original complex were ideal for refugees following the 1906 disaster, as indicated by photographs from the period. *Landmark Number 58*

HASLETT WAREHOUSE

680 Beach Street

The building now known as the Haslett Warehouse was built as a warehouse for the adjacent cannery. The architect was William Mooser, Jr., who was also responsible for many of the buildings in Ghirardelli Square. It was completed in 1909. Although a twentieth-century structure, the building exemplifies the genre of nineteenth-century warehouses, which were once predominant in the northern waterfront area of San Francisco. Because many have been razed, this building at this location is of considerable significance. Located opposite the terminus of the Hyde Street cable car, it establishes the character of the area as it once was for those arriving by cable car. It calls to mind past waterfront uses and sets the standard for scale and proportion in the area, and its straightforward expression of brick as a building material serves as a preview of other remaining historic masonry buildings found in the vicinity. The Haslett Warehouse is listed on the National Register. *Landmark Number 59*

Hunter's Point Springs and Albion Brewery

881 Innes Avenue

Piper House

(Sylvester House) 1556 Revere Avenue

The Albion Ale and Porter Brewery was founded in 1870 by John Hamlin Burnell. A supply of fresh water was a critical ingredient for developing a brewery, and Burnell found this in abundance in the underground springs beneath the property. The structure housing the brewery covered fully half of the site originally, although little remains today but the reconstructed main brewery building. This stone building with its three-story towers was probably modeled after the Norman castles of England. It is said that the original buildings were built by English stonemasons, commissioned by Burnell, using rock hewn from nearby Bayview Hill. *Landmark Number 60*

The house was built in about 1865 by Stephen L. Piper, a prominent carpenter and house builder in the southern portion of San Francisco now known as the Bayview District. The Sylvesters, for whom the building is named, resided in the house from 1884 to 1900. At that time the house was located on the south side of Sumatra near Savannah Street. In 1913 the house was moved to its present location on Revere Street. The basement, added at the time of the move, was constructed from the stables on the previous site. The Sylvesters were butchers and cattle dealers at a time when this district was set aside by state law as "Butchertown." The building is typical of a country Victorian Italianate, with its broad, expansive front porch. *Landmark Number 61*

MISH HOUSE
1153 Oak Street

This house was built in about 1885 as a single-family residence for Mrs. Sarah Mish, a pioneer who had a dressmaking and millinery business in San Francisco. Her husband, Phenes, was a well-known merchant from the 1850s to the 1880s. There is some confusion about the original location of the house. It was probably moved from 407 Divisadero Street to its current address in 1898 to make way for retail stores and multiple dwellings, which were then built upon the original site. An early photograph indicates that the house was very elegant for its day. Its original mansard roof and elaborate entrance stair (both probably removed when the building was relocated) made the exterior one of the finer products of the house builder's art in the era of the San Francisco Victorian (see also Landmark No. 32). *Landmark Number 62*

QUINN HOUSE
1562 McKinnon Avenue

(Not Pictured) As one of the oldest and most attractive residences in the Bayview District, this two-story frame house possesses an architectural style and quality that enhances the community's visual environment. Although the date of construction is unknown, the house was occupied as early as 1875 by Mrs. Mary Quinn. It remained in the ownership of the Quinn family for more than eighty years. This house occupies an unusual place in the annals of San Francisco Victoriana as one of the earlier and more simplified of the Italianate Style. As a Victorian, it might be considered a study in modesty. *Landmark Number 63*

FLOOD MANSION

(Pacific Union Club)

1000 California Street

Designed by Augustus Laver, this mansion originally served as the town house for James Clair Flood, one of the Nevada Comstock mining kings. Completed in 1886, it was the first brownstone west of the Mississippi and the only Nob Hill palace to survive the disaster of 1906. The fire devastated all the other Nob Hill mansions because they were constructed of wood. Although the interior of this building was gutted, the stone shell remained, and it was sold to the Pacific Union Club in 1907. The commission to redesign the mansion as a club was given to prominent San Francisco architect Willis Polk, who added a third floor and the semicircular wings. Brownstone from Connecticut was brought from the original quarry to harmonize with the existing stone.

This building is listed on the National Register and has been designated a National Historic Landmark by the United States Department of the Interior. *Landmark Number 64*

TRINITY EPISCOPAL CHURCH

1668 Bush Street

The present church was designed by architect A. Page Brown in 1892 for a congregation that dates from 1849. This building stood unscathed through the 1906 disaster. Included among its many decorative features are a small angel and one stained-glass window, both by Louis Tiffany. Massive in effect, the architecture is Norman in style, modeled on Durham Cathedral. The church is built of rough-hewn Colusa sandstone. Restoration work was completed in 1962. *Landmark Number 65*

TANFORAN COTTAGES
214 and 220 Dolores Street

STANYAN HOUSE
2006 Bush Street

Considered to be the oldest extant residential buildings in the Mission District, these cottages are most commonly associated with the Tanforan ranching family. Both are built of redwood. Differences in their architectural styling suggest that 214 Dolores is the older of the two. They are located on what was originally a portion of Francisco Guerrero's Mexican Land Grant of 1836.

These cottages were part of an urbanization process: They were built at a time when the Mission was being developed as a resort haven for downtown San Francisco. Subsequently, many of San Francisco's large Victorian mansions were built in this district, which was valued for its particularly good climate. The similarities to New England houses of the period suggest these buildings were either designed by a newly arrived architect from the East or copied from a book. *Landmark Numbers 67 and 68*

The Stanyan House is one of the oldest in the city. It remained in the Stanyan family for more than 110 years, which is undoubtedly why it survived. The Stanyan family believes the building was built in 1854 and that Charles Stanyan purchased it some six months after it was completed. The family also owned the cottage around the corner at 1907 Buchanan, which was moved to that site in 1875.

It was a prefabricated house, shipped around Cape Horn from Boston, and the architectural style reflects its more severe New England origins in its simplicity and austerity, qualities that distinguish it from its later, more flamboyant Victorian neighbors. *Landmark Number 66*

HAAS-LILIENTHAL HOUSE

2007 Franklin Street

The Haas-Lilienthal House is one of only two house-museums in San Francisco (the other being Landmark No. 17). Built in 1885, this residence was designed by architect Peter R. Schmidt for prominent businessman William Haas. In 1917 it became the home of his daughter Alice and her husband, Samuel Lilienthal. She continued to live in the house until her death in 1972. The house was then donated by her heirs to the Foundation for San Francisco's Architectural Heritage, which operates the property in its role as a community trust; public tours of the main floors are available. An addition to the building was done in 1928 by then-prominent architect Gardiner Dailey. This residence is listed on the National Register of Historic Places, and the National Trust for Historic Preservation holds a façade easement on the property. *Landmark Number 69*

ATHERTON HOUSE

1990 California Street

EMERIC BUILDING

(Goodman Building) 1117 Geary Street

This house was built in 1881 for Mrs. Faxon Dean Atherton after the death of her husband, for whom the town of Atherton, south of San Francisco, is named. A native of Dedham, Massachusetts, Mr. Atherton played a significant role in the commercial history of California.

After changing ownership many times, the building was purchased in 1923 by architect Charles J. Rousseau, under whose direction it was divided into thirteen dwelling units, which is how it remains today. The building is eclectic and even bizarre in conception; its dominant architectural styles are Queen Anne and Stick-Eastlake. *Landmark Number 70*

In 1869, French immigrant Joseph Emeric erected a residential structure on this site. In 1899, his granddaughter sold the building to Abraham and Sarah Goodman, recent arrivals from New York, who maintained a tailoring business and residence in the building. The structure survived the 1906 disaster and soon thereafter underwent major remodeling, presumably to accommodate the newly emerging needs of the city. From that time it has served variously as a hotel, offices, and in the 1970s, as work and living space for an artists' collective. *Landmark Number 71*

MORRIS STORE

(Circle Gallery)

140 Maiden Lane

An alteration to an existing 1911 warehouse, this is one of the most modern and striking buildings in San Francisco. Built in 1948 as a specialty retail store, this Frank Lloyd Wright structure is clearly the work of a master, and it stands today as a tribute to Wright's genius. After the Hallidie Building (Landmark No. 37), it is probably San Francisco's most important modern building. Its curving interior is seen as a precursor to Wright's Guggenheim Museum. The banners in the photograph are the addition of the current occupant. *Landmark Number 72*

MILLS BUILDING AND TOWER

220 Montgomery Street and 220 Bush Street

The Mills Building stands as San Francisco's only intact example of the Chicago School of architecture. It was designed in 1890 by the famous Chicago architectural firm of Burnham and Root. The building suffered only minor damage to the exterior in 1906, but the interior was badly damaged by fire. It was rebuilt in 1907 under the direction of Willis Polk. At that time, the building was also extended along Bush Street. In 1914, and again in 1918, vertical additions were made to the building, bringing it to its current height of ten stories. In 1931, the adjoining Mills Tower was built to the design of Lewis Hobart, who developed a treatment that is considered very compatible with the original structure. The building carries the name of its builder, Darius Ogden Mills, a millionaire banker and noted philanthropist. *Landmark Number 76*

LOTTA'S FOUNTAIN

Pedestrian island,
Northeast corner of Geary, Market, and Kearny Streets

On September 9, 1875, the twenty-fifth anniversary of California statehood, this elaborate public drinking fountain was formally presented to the city. It was the gift of the famed entertainer Lotta Crabtree, who made her debut in San Francisco and always held the city in high regard. It has been the scene of many public gatherings, the most significant occurring on Christmas Eve, 1910, when Mme Luisa Tetrazzini sang before a crowd estimated at 250,000.

The fountain was designed by architects Wyneken and Townsend and is listed on the National Register. *Landmark Number 73*

Samuels Clock

856 Market Street

The city's most famous street clock made its appearance in front of the Albert S. Samuels Jewelry Company on Market Street concurrent with the February 1915 opening of the Panama-Pacific International Exposition. The clock was designed and built by Samuels in collaboration with Joseph Mayer, a mechanical engineer from Seattle. *Landmark Number 77*

Stone House
1348 South Van Ness Avenue

Whittier Mansion
(California Historical Society)
2090 Jackson Street

This luxurious house was commissioned by attorney Frank M. Stone in 1886 as his private residence. It was designed by architect Seth Babson. Stone, the son of a New England attorney, arrived in California in 1874. He became a prominent member of the California Bar.

In its architectural styling, the Stone residence illustrates the transition from the Stick to the Queen Anne Style; its principal elements and massing are typically the latter, while its detailing is more representative of the former. *Landmark Number 74*

The mansion was designed in 1894 by Edward R. Swain as a private residence for widower William Franklin Whittier and his children. Whittier began his career in a paint firm, which led to his founding the Fuller-O'Brien Paint Company.

The Whittier house was built at a time when the fashions of the later nineteenth century were beginning to give way to more correct period styling. Thus, the general massing of the structure, with its strongly emphasized circular towers, is both Queen Anne and Romanesque Revival. The rigid symmetry of the façade suggests a new interest in formality that contrasts with the late-nineteenth-century fascination with asymmetry and the picturesque. The Classical portico, using the Ionic order, represents a return to period sources, which became a national style in the 1890s. *Landmark Number 75*

MERRILL CONSERVATORY

(Sunnyside Conservatory)
220 Monterey Boulevard

The Sunnyside Conservatory is one of the most unusual structures in the Mission District. This handsome and utilitarian 1918 wooden structure was constructed by Frank Merrill, an inventor and inveterate stargazer. In the gardens behind the late Victorian house on the property, Merrill built a steel observatory tower (still standing), which revolved on steel balls. His interest in rare plants and birds led to construction of the conservatory. His daring plunge into the aircraft business led to his financial ruin, and in 1919 the bank sold his property, which included the conservatory and six of the eight original lots. As evidenced by the photograph, the building has been partially restored (the glass has been removed due to vandalism). The building was purchased by the city for rehabilitation and use as a public park. *Landmark Number 78*

MILLER-JOOST HOUSE
3224 Market Street

CLARKE MANSION
(Nobby Clarke's Folly) 250 Douglass Street

The date of construction of the Miller-Joost House may be as early as 1867, at the time of the subdivision of the San Miguel Rancho. It was apparently designed and built by Adam Miller, the original occupant, who was a German immigrant. Trained as both an architect and carpenter, Miller supported himself in California as a dairy farmer. Miller's daughter Anna and her husband, Behrend Joost, subsequently occupied the house.

The Miller-Joost House is not typical of San Francisco houses in that it was built as a freestanding structure over one hundred years ago and remains so to this day. Designed as a suburban residence, the house retains that characteristic on its ample lot. While no particular architectural idiom may be ascribed to it, most of its windows indicate the Italianate influences of the late 1860s and 70s. *Landmark Number 79*

When this imposing structure was completed in 1891, it was situated on the easterly boundary of a 17-acre tract owned by its builder, Alfred E. "Nobby" Clarke. The mansion was dubbed "Clarke's folly" and was occupied by him for only about five years. The building is a fitting memorial for Clarke, whose character was as flamboyant and eccentric as the residence he constructed. A colorful attorney, Clarke received a great deal of publicity during his lifetime.

In terms of styling, the building is best described as eclectic, which in this case combines popular architectural features of the waning Queen Anne epoch (three round towers) with elements of the emerging Classical Revival. *Landmark Number 80*

Ohabai Shalome Temple
(Bush Street Temple)
1881 Bush Street

Columbia Theater
(Geary Theater)
415 Geary Street

This structure was designed by Moses J. Lyon in 1895 to serve as a house of worship for the third congregation of San Francisco Jews, a congregation that dates from 1864. While commonly known as the Bush Street Temple, its Hebrew name was Ohabai Shalome, which translates as "Lovers of Peace." As seen today, the temple features delicate Venetian tracery along with elements of both Romanesque and Moorish architecture. All of these elements are typical of synagogue architecture, although they have rarely been combined in such a lively ensemble.

The bracing between the towers was designed to support an intricate display of Judaic symbols, including tablets, subsequently removed, that represented the Ten Commandments. Tall spires, which lent an even more exotic appearance to the original structure, have also been removed. *Landmark Number 81*

The Columbia Theater was built in 1910 to the designs of Bliss and Faville, who were prominent San Francisco architects. Gottlob and Marx commissioned the building to replace a previous Columbia Theater destroyed in 1906. The theater housed legendary performances by most of the stage luminaries of the period, and it continues that tradition today as the home of the American Conservatory Theater. The theater's interior sustained major damage during the 1989 earthquake, requiring substantial restoration work.

Aside from its important Neoclassical brick and terra-cotta façade, the building is blessed with perfect acoustics, which is credited as the reason it has survived when so many theaters of its vintage have fallen to the wrecker's ball. It is listed on the National Register. *Landmark Number 82*

War Memorial
Opera House
and
Veterans Building

Van Ness Avenue between Grove and McAllister Streets

Since 1911, San Franciscans envisioned a replacement for the opera houses lost to the 1906 earthquake and fire, but it was not until 1923 that the city really began the process of building the Opera House and its twin Veterans Building. In that year, architects Arthur Brown, Jr., and G. Albert Lansburgh were commissioned to design the War Memorial. Construction began in 1931, with the first performance taking place on October 15, 1932.

Not only one of the great opera houses of the world, San Francisco's Opera House also hosted the formation of the United Nations in 1945 and the signing of the peace treaty with Japan in 1951. The Opera House and Veterans Building, together with the courtyard between them, form an integral complex designed to complement and enhance City Hall (also designed by Brown). This Civic Center landmark is the last of the great Beaux-Arts projects. The entire complex is a National Register Historic District and has been proposed as a local Historic District. *Landmark Number 84*

St. John's Presbyterian Church
25 Lake Street

The site of this church was selected to house a congregation that dates from 1870. Architects Dodge and Dolliver were commissioned to design the building, which held its first services on April 15, 1906. Three days later the building was severely damaged by the earthquake. On April 28, 1907, repairs complete, the formal dedication was held. Arthur Foster, St. John's patron, turned over the deed to the congregation with the admonition, "To be rich in spirit and free of debt," a goal the church maintains to this day.

Architecturally, the structure is an almost exact replication of the congregation's original building, constructed sometime before 1870 as St. James Episcopal Church. *Landmark Number 83*

CALIFORNIA SCHOOL OF FINE ARTS

(San Francisco Art Institute) 800 Chestnut Street

This building was designed in 1926 by architects Bakewell and Brown for the San Francisco Art Association to house the California School of Fine Arts. Now the San Francisco Art Institute, this school has figured prominently in the arts community since it was first established in 1871.

The building is modified Spanish Colonial Revival, with walls of stripped concrete, stained a soft adobe color. Multileveled red tile roofs are skylighted to provide natural sunlight for the studios within, and a bell tower rises above the patio in the style of the Spanish missions. An addition was built to the rear in the late 1960s. In this photograph the bell tower is adorned with a student's artwork. *Landmark Number 85*

POTRERO HILL
NEIGHBORHOOD HOUSE
953 De Haro Street

The Potrero Hill Neighborhood House was established in 1919 by the Presbyterian Church to provide services to newly arriving Russian immigrants who were settling in the area. Similar neighborhood houses, which served as havens for newcomers, were established across the country, helping to integrate foreigners into the American way of life. Designed by the prominent architect Julia Morgan, the low, rambling structure, without architectural pretensions, is characteristic of much of Morgan's work. The shingled building conforms to the contours of its hillside site, and its many broad windows offer a grand view of the city. *Landmark Number 86*

Jessie Street Substation

220 Jessie Street

Firehouse, Engine Company No. 21

1152 Oak Street

(See page 8) This aesthetically outstanding example of early-twentieth-century Classical Revivalism was designed by one of the Bay Area's most talented architects, Willis Polk. It is the prototypical application of a style developed for Pacific Gas & Electric Company in their long-term contribution to the City Beautiful Movement in San Francisco, which made civic ornaments of industrial structures. The original plain brick building, which had some Romanesque detailing fronting on Stevenson Street, was built in 1881. A Polk addition was completed in 1907, giving the building a wonderful, if strange, asymmetrical front elevation.

Pictured is a detail over a secondary entrance of a group of cherubs holding garlands of fruit and gourds beneath a torch, done in a Baroque style. *Landmark Number 87*

Typical of its counterparts from a bygone era, this firehouse recalls a time when buildings for municipal services were designed not only to fulfill a utilitarian purpose but to complement visually the neighborhoods. So highly esteemed are these old firehouses that when they become obsolete, people vie for the opportunity to restore and rehabilitate them for other uses. Built in 1893 by R. Doyle & Sons, to the designs of architects Henriksen and Mahoney, this firehouse is very nearly a twin to one at 3022 Washington Street (Landmark No. 93). It also forms a complement to the adjacent historic area, which includes the Phelps and Mish houses (Landmark Nos. 32 and 62, respectively). *Landmark Number 89*

FIREHOUSE, ENGINE COMPANY No. 23

3022 Washington Street

Like many nineteenth-century buildings that were designed to be useful rather than decorative, this firehouse has dignity and style expressed in the simplest of terms: good proportions, big space, and handsome woodwork. These are all qualities that are hard to duplicate today. Constructed in 1893, it is one of three that were designed by Henriksen and Mahoney. The other two are 1152 Oak Street (Landmark No. 89) and 2545 Folsom Street, now demolished. Used as a firehouse until 1963, the building was purchased by the famous interior designer the late John Dickenson, who converted it into his design studio and residence. In 1970 the restoration of many missing exterior architectural details was completed. *Landmark Number 93*

PALACE OF FINE ARTS

(Reconstruction)

Baker between Bay and Jefferson Streets

The Palace of Fine Arts holds a special place in the hearts of San Franciscans. Designed by the preeminent Berkeley architect Bernard Maybeck, it was erected as a temporary building in 1914 for the Panama-Pacific International Exposition. Visitors were captivated by its beauty, and efforts were immediately undertaken to have it reconstructed of permanent materials. But half a century would pass before this was accomplished.

The reconstruction of the Palace of Fine Arts, financed in part by philanthropist Walter S. Johnson, necessitated its total demolition except for the galleries housed in the curvilinear building to the rear of the colonnade. While the colonnade and rotunda are virtual reproductions of the original, the architectural treatment of the galleries was simplified for economic reasons. *Landmark Number 88*

Ferry Building

The Embarcadero at Market Street

Although other San Francisco buildings lay claim to greater age, the most readily identifiable building in San Francisco is the Ferry Building. In many ways it serves as a symbol for the entire region. Since its completion in 1903, it undoubtedly has been viewed by more people than any other building in the history of the city.

The design of the building was begun in 1894 by A. Page Brown, who died in 1896 before it was completed. Willis Polk, Bernard Maybeck, and A. C. Schweinforth worked in Brown's office during this period. Schweinforth appears to be the designer of the building, although the construction was supervised by Edward R. Swain. The structure's most prominent feature is the tower, which rises 235 feet and is visible for much of the length of Market Street. It is modeled after the Giralda of the Cathedral of Seville and resembles the 1890 version of Madison Square Garden, which was designed by McKim, Mead & White, the architectural firm in which Brown did his apprenticeship. *Landmark Number 90*

GIBB-SANBORN WAREHOUSE, SOUTH

(Trinidad Bean and Elevator Company)

855 Front Street

GIBB-SANBORN WAREHOUSE, NORTH

(Pelican Paper Company)

901 Front Street

The two Gibb-Sanborn warehouses are among a handful of extant San Francisco structures that date from the Gold Rush era; they probably were built in 1855 by forty-niner Daniel Gibb, a commission merchant who was active in civic affairs. As evidenced by an early lithograph and later photographs, they were rebuilt along their original lines following extensive earthquake damage in 1906. *Landmark Numbers 91 and 92*

PANTAGES THEATER BUILDING

(Orpheum Theater Building)
1192 Market Street

Possessing the most impressive theater façade on Market Street, the Pantages Theater was erected in 1926. It was designed by B. Marcus Priteca, a West Coast theater architect, to serve as a showcase for the Pantages vaudeville chain. In the 1930s, the Orpheum, as it then became known, was converted into a movie theater. In 1953 it was renovated to house Cinerama. In the mid-sixties the theater was dark, except for occasional special events. In the late seventies, the building became the home of the San Francisco Civic Light Opera, and it is currently a thriving theater once again. *Landmark Number 94*

FRANCIS SCOTT KEY
MONUMENT
Music Concourse, Golden Gate Park

The Francis Scott Key Monument bears the distinction of having been the first in the United States to memorialize the author of "The Star-Spangled Banner." The monument was commissioned by San Francisco philanthropist James Lick. Erected in 1888, it was designed by sculptor William W. Story. Although this was some seventy-four years after Key wrote the poem, it was not until 1931 that Congress adopted the melody and lyrics as the official national anthem. The monument was damaged in 1906 and, after repairs, it was moved to another position in the park. In 1967 it was again restored, and relocated to the site it currently occupies. *Landmark Number 96*

KOSHLAND HOUSE

(Le Petit Trianon)

3800 Washington Street

The Koshland House, its Washington Street façade patterned after the south face of the Petit Trianon at Versailles, was built for the Marcus Koshlands in 1902 from the designs of Frank S. Van Trees. Koshland was a native San Franciscan and prominent in the business community. His wife, also a native, was active in the city's cultural life for over sixty years.

The building features a central atrium, three stories high, which brings light into most of the interior rooms. The main hall at the bottom of the atrium is ringed by green Irish marble columns with bronze capitals and bases. The basement features an elaborate French-style mirrored ballroom that can accommodate sit-down dinners for more than one hundred guests, served from an adjacent commercial-size kitchen.

The Koshland House is listed on the National Register. *Landmark Number 95*

ATKINSON HOUSE
1302 Broadway

Among San Francisco's oldest homes, the Atkinson House was built in 1853 by Joseph M. Atkinson, a brick contractor, as his residence, and later his office. It is remarkable that the dwelling, located within walking distance of the city's original settlement at Yerba Buena Cove, has survived for 138 years. The house still stands today, a free-standing structure in one of San Francisco's most densely populated areas.

Reminiscent of an Italian villa, the building was remodeled by Willis Polk around 1900. After a fire in 1931, it was once again remodeled or restored. No apparent changes have occurred since that time. *Landmark Number 97*

ORIENTAL WAREHOUSE

650 First Street

The Oriental Warehouse, built in 1867, is all that remains in San Francisco of the Pacific Mail Steamship Company, a firm whose activities had considerable impact historically, economically, and socially on the nation, the state, and the city. The Pacific Mail Steamship Company initially carried mail, passengers, treasure, and cargo on a regular schedule between Panama and Gold Rush San Francisco. Later, the firm was the first line to establish regular mail, passenger, and trade service between this country and the Orient. It carried thousands of Asians, mostly Chinese, who became the source of cheap labor to build railroads and develop California's agricultural business. This importation continued until the Exclusion Act of 1882. The presence of these workers, often exploited and commonly considered a threat by Caucasian job-seekers, led to social, labor, and economic changes whose effects are still felt today.

Freestanding, and surrounded by recent residential development, the Oriental Warehouse, though suffering from both fire and earthquake damage, still survives as a mute but eloquent reminder of San Francisco's earliest period. *Landmark Number 101*

ORTMAN-SHUMATE HOUSE

1901 Scott Street

On the northwest corner of Scott and Pine streets stands a stately Italianate residence that was built in 1870 and has been continuously occupied by the same family for 121 years. The site is of particular interest for its extensive gardens, a rarity in San Francisco. The house has been modified over time to meet the changing needs of its owners, but each alteration has been done with rare sensitivity; the changes are not visible to anyone unfamiliar with the building's original appearance. *Landmark Number 98*

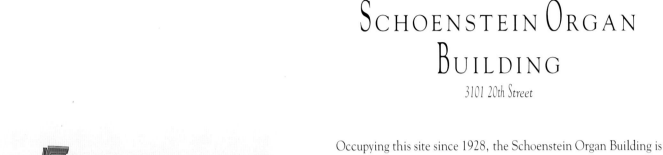

SCHOENSTEIN ORGAN BUILDING

3101 20th Street

Occupying this site since 1928, the Schoenstein Organ Building is the place of business for one of the oldest organ firms in the country, and one of the oldest industrial concerns in San Francisco. The Schoenstein family has been building pipe organs since 1850, beginning in their native Germany. The family came to San Francisco in 1868 and established an organ business in 1877.

The current building exists in an extraordinary state of preservation. Except for the "band room," no detail of the building has been altered, and it is the intention of the current owner that the building remain unchanged. *Landmark Number 99*

CASTRO THEATER

429 Castro Street

The Castro Theater is an exceptionally fine example of 1920s movie-theater design and represents a major early work of one of San Francisco's most important architectural firms, Miller and Pflueger. It was one of the first and finest major theaters built by San Francisco's oldest movie-business family, the Nassers. To this day, the Castro remains essentially unaltered, both inside and out. *Landmark Number 100*

ITALIAN SWISS COLONY WAREHOUSE

1265 Battery Street

The Italian Swiss Colony Warehouse, built in 1903 from designs by Hemenway and Miller, ranks as one of the finest examples of warehouse architecture remaining in San Francisco's Northeast Waterfront Historic District. Once commonplace throughout the area, many of the warehouses have been demolished. However, the few that remain reveal the handsome qualities that typified these buildings and asserted a pride of ownership. As its name implies, this building was constructed for an organization whose founders had Italian origins, and the façades on Battery and Greenwich streets suggest the palazzi of their homeland. This building underwent extensive alterations in the 1980s when it became part of the corporate headquarters for Levi Strauss & Co. *Landmark Number 102*

MARKET STREET RAILWAY SUBSTATION

1190 Fillmore Street

One of the first and largest substations, this one at Turk and Fillmore streets was built near the turn of the century, when San Francisco's street railways were converted to electric power. When it ceased operations, it was one of the last old-time street-railway substations still in regular use in western America. The structure, a handsome example of the brick-and-sandstone architecture of the time, stood through the disaster of 1906 and was essential in making the Fillmore Street line the first to be put back into service.

The building suffered some damage in the October 1989 earthquake. *Landmark Number 105*

CHAMBORD APARTMENTS

1298 Sacramento Street

The Chambord apartment house, with its unusual French Beaux-Arts Style architecture has always intrigued the casual passerby. Despite the removal of some of its original exterior embellishments, its intrinsic flamboyance continues to delight the eye and mark the corner on the crest of the hill.

The building was commissioned in 1921 by James Witt Dougherty and designed by James Francis Dunn, who did not live to see the building completed. Dunn was heavily influenced by French architecture, and most of his work derived from this style. *Landmark Number 106*

Calvary Presbyterian Church

2501 Fillmore Street

Calvary Church's unique, stately, and graceful architectural features include rounded, opalescent-lavender stained-glass windows whose rich hue is most evident when the sun strikes them. Built between 1900 and 1902, the building is the work of architects Charles and George McDougall. The building is the third home for Calvary, a congregation that has existed since 1854. The church is in the Edwardian Style, which combines Renaissance and Neo-classical forms with some Gothic elements. This was the style that succeeded the Victorian in San Francisco. *Landmark Number 103*

INDEPENDENT WOOD COMPANY
1105 Battery Street

This small, unpretentious building is a pleasant reminder of the seafaring activities that once dominated the northern waterfront. Although buildings of this type were commonplace, this is one of the few remaining that were originally constructed for ground-floor retail use with lodgings above catering to seamen. The building was erected in 1907 by E. J. Brandon for the Independent Wood Company, dealers in "wood, ties, posts, tanbark, etc." The offices of the company occupied the lower floor with the stock-in-trade in open storage on the remainder of the lot. The upper floor was used for lodging.

Today, the building houses a bank and is part of the large Levi Strauss & Co. World Headquarters complex, some of which is cantilevered over this small historic structure. *Landmark Number 104*

RINCON ANNEX POST OFFICE

Spear and Mission Streets

The Rincon Annex to the United States Post Office was designed by Gilbert Underwood and built in 1939 by the George A. Fuller Construction Company. It is one of the finest San Francisco examples of a large public building in the Streamline Moderne Style. Sponsored by the W.P.A., it is a superb period piece in mint condition.

The building is also well known and highly regarded for its interior murals, painted over eight years by artist Anton Refregier. The murals are important not only for their size but also for the sweep of their narrative power and for the controversy caused by their content, which, some thought, espoused Communist philosophy. Ninety-one changes were required before final approval was given by the Federal government. The building is listed on the National Register at the National Level of Significance. *Landmark Number 107*

STATE ARMORY AND ARSENAL

1800 Mission Street

For fifty-eight years, the Armory was home to the San Francisco National Guard. Somewhat forbidding, with its dark fortress-like appearance, the building is entrenched four-square at the corner of Mission and 14th streets. It almost overpowers the skeptical observer, implying that its function on this particular corner has been of no less importance than that of Fort Point, which guards the entrance to the Golden Gate. Built in 1914, to the plans of Los Angeles architects Woollett and Woollett, the building is visually striking in the context of its neighborhood. *Landmark Number 108*

BOREL BUILDING
440 Montgomery Street

The A. Borel & Company Building was designed by Albert Pissis and constructed for Antoine Borel, banker and diplomat, in 1908. Borel is generally thought of as a banking company, although it was apparently more of an investment firm than a commercial bank. This small two-story granite building echoes the Beaux-Arts-inspired "commercial classicism" so strongly evident in the reconstruction of San Francisco following 1906. *Landmark Number 109*

ITALIAN AMERICAN BANK BUILDING
(Coast Savings)
460 Montgomery Street

The Italian American Bank Building replaced one destroyed by the 1906 earthquake. Designed by the famous architect John Galen Howard, it is considered to be an excellent example of the banking-temple style of the era.

Both this building and its neighbor, the Borel Building, were virtually demolished to make way for a high-rise office building, which appears to be precariously perched between and above them. In actuality, only the front façade of the Borel Building and the front and one side façade of the Italian American Bank Building remain intact. It is projects such as this that give rise to the term "facadomy." *Landmark Number 110*

Family Service Agency

1010 Gough Street

Bernard Maybeck, one of the Bay Area's most important architects, created a humane, comfortable scale in this fairly large institutional building. The picturesque, asymmetrical massing of geometric elements, with balconies, trellises, and landscaping, contributes to a domestic character that relates to a once largely residential neighborhood. Simplicity of ornamentation, arched openings, and a tile roof mark its Spanish Colonial antecedents, transformed by the sure hand of a master architect into an original work. The building was designed in conjunction with the agency director, Kitty Felton, who challenged Maybeck to develop a building that "must show forth the spirit of its work." That spirit included many advanced social programs now routinely used throughout the United States. Maybeck answered the challenge with a building that still functions effectively and that, in Felton's words, "has expressed that outreaching of human sympathy, that reverence for personality which is the inspiration for all service." *Landmark Number 111*

BELT LINE RAILROAD ROUNDHOUSE

The Embarcadero at Lombard and Sansome Streets

The 1914 Belt Line Roundhouse is the only roundhouse ever built in San Francisco. The belt line system served the docks lining The Embarcadero. In 1923, Harbor Commissioner Edward Murphy observed, "One of San Francisco's unique and most important services, and one that distinguishes it from practically every other great port on the Western continent, is the efficiency of its Belt Railroad, so called, whereby every pier and practically every berth alongside is connected directly with the railway systems of America."

The Roundhouse building is a rare example of a structure whose form derives solely from its functional requirements. It is totally devoid of the decorative elements usually associated with even the most utilitarian buildings of the period. As such, it is a significant forerunner of the structural expressionism that was to become a major concern in International Style architecture. A compatible office building was added to the compound recently when the Roundhouse itself was converted to office use. *Landmark Number 114*

ROTHCHILD HOUSE

964 Eddy Street

(*Not Pictured*) This building is a fine example of an 1880 restrained Italianate residence. It was once part of a row of houses cited by the San Francisco Redevelopment Agency for rehabilitation due to their exceptional architectural and historical merit. It has been well restored and reconverted to its original single-family use by its present owner. Henriette Rothchild, daughter of the original owner, Hugo Rothchild, was the first wife of the distinguished California anthropologist Alfred Kroeber. The building recently suffered major fire damage and is currently undergoing restoration. *Landmark Number 112*

SAN FRANCISCO MINING EXCHANGE

350 Bush Street

This building is the last visible remnant of the San Francisco Mining Exchange. Before its dissolution in 1967, it was the second-oldest exchange in the United States, after the New York Stock Exchange.

The building, a 1923 work of architects Miller and Pflueger, has a close and probably deliberate resemblance to the New York Stock Exchange. Its monumental façade, with ornamental details from early Greek and Roman models, has a pediment group of five figures representing the gods of Parnassus, by sculptor Jo Moro. *Landmark Number 113*

LANE LIBRARY

(Health Sciences Library)

2395 Sacramento Street

The work of Albert Pissis, San Francisco's first architect trained at the Ecole des Beaux-Arts, the Health Sciences Library is a classic example of his restrained and balanced Beaux-Arts style. The origins of the institutions with which the building is connected date from the 1858 founding by Dr. Elias S. Cooper of the first medical school in the West. This 1912 building is dedicated to the physicians and dentists who made an important contribution to San Francisco's medical history. Of particular note are the murals in the reading room, which were executed by Arthur Mathews. *Landmark Number 115*

St. Paulus Lutheran Church

999 Eddy Street

The soaring verticality of the Gothic Style, here executed in wood, makes this church more than hold its own in a neighborhood of churches more imposing in size. Its history is an old one, and the church has served the city in time of need. Although its congregation has changed over the years, the church has remained in service, with virtually no alterations to the exterior since it was built in 1894. The building is attributed to architect Julius A. Kraft. *Landmark Number 116*

HAMMERSMITH BUILDING
301 Sutter Street

Although it occupies one of the smallest sites in the retail area, the Hammersmith Building makes a contribution to the streetscape that is disproportionate to its size. This important corner building characterizes, in its own immediate area, the Beaux-Arts–inspired post-1906 development of much of the downtown. The building has a large amount of glass for its era and employs the striking motif of building-wide arches covering each street façade. It has maintained its integrity, having been little remodeled since it was built in 1907. Its architect, G. Albert Lansburgh, became known for his theater designs and was later asked, along with Arthur Brown, Jr., to design the Opera House (Landmark No. 84). *Landmark Number 117*

CHEVRA MIKVAH ISRAEL
AND
B'NAI DAVID SYNAGOGUE
3535 19th Street

(Not Pictured) Chevra Mikvah Israel and B'nai David Synagogue are the last remaining evidence of a once-large Jewish population in the Mission District. The mikvah (ritual bath) was the first to be located in California. Immigrants said to be responsible for the building of this structure (1880–1925) came from the "Pale of Settlement" areas of Poland, Russia, and Romania. The dispersal of this Orthodox Jewish community beginning in the 1930s and 40s, coupled with the requirement that Orthodox Jews walk to prayer, caused the membership gradually to decline until regular services ceased in 1976. The Mission District is rich in late-nineteenth and early-twentieth-century houses of worship, but this synagogue is unique for its mikvah, not only in the Mission, but in all of San Francisco. No longer a synagogue, B'nai David has recently been converted to condominiums. *Landmark Number 118*

CHAMBERS MANSION

(Mansion Hotel) 2220 Sacramento Street

This building is an interesting example of Queen Anne architecture, executed by prominent architect-builder J. C. Mathews and Son. After it was inherited by two nieces of the original owner, the house was substantially altered under the direction of architect Houghton Sawyer. The house was originally built in the 1880s for Utah State Senator Richard Craig Chambers, one of the richest and most powerful men in the intermountain region. He made his fortune in the interior and built his town house in the local regional metropolis, San Francisco. *Landmark Number 119*

St. Joseph's Church, Rectory, Parish House, and Garden

1415 Howard

St. Joseph's Church and Parish were founded in 1861 by the Reverand Hugh Gallagher under the direction of California's first archbishop, Joseph Alemany. The original frame structure proved inadequate for the increasing number of parishioners and was replaced with a more substantial structure, which was destroyed in 1906. The present church was dedicated in 1914. St. Joseph's Parish responded to the city's vital need for education with the establishment of two schools in 1867, one each for girls and boys. There have been educational facilities at the site since that time.

St. Joseph's Church and complex, with its beautifully maintained grounds, has been important to many groups. It continues to reflect social and economic changes in the city, and exemplifies church involvement in the evolving sociological conditions of an urban center as illustrated by the shift from the original Irish congregation to today's parishioners, who are mostly immigrants from the Philippines. *Landmark Number 120*

JULIUS' CASTLE

302 Greenwich Street

A unique building, Julius' Castle is a well-known visual landmark on the northeast cliff of Telegraph Hill. Italian architect Louis Mastropasqua planned it in 1923 to recall an earlier castle that stood nearby from 1882 to 1903. The new castle also reflected Mastropasqua's Arts and Crafts Movement background. The restaurant became a favorite with celebrities in entertainment, politics, and business, and it survives as a living page from the history of the local Italian community. *Landmark Number 121*

CLAY STREET CENTER AND RESIDENCE CLUB

(Chinatown YWCA) 965 Clay Street

The founding of the Clay Street Center was the result of a collaborative effort between missionaries and Chinese community members who saw the need for social services among Chinese women. It was designed by pioneering woman architect Julia Morgan, who had many firsts to her credit: she was the first woman to graduate in engineering from the University of California at Berkeley, the first woman to study at the Ecole des Beaux-Arts, and the first woman architect to be licensed in California. The Clay Street Center and Residence Club reflected the era when women first sought equal rights and entered the world of men, while the Chinese YWCA, which now occupies the building, reflects a similar process in the socialization of the Chinese into American traditions. Built in 1932, the building is an excellent example of Morgan's high-quality work. She was the most important woman architect in America, known primarily for her work with William Randolph Hearst on his castle, San Simeon. *Landmark Number 122*

McMullen House
827 Guerrero Street

This house was built in 1881 (with additions as late as 1906) and is an impressive structure in its own right. It is even more important, however, as an example of the evolution of domestic architecture in the late nineteenth century. Beginning as a simple early-Victorian cottage, it was enlarged by noted architect Samuel Newsom into an elegant tower house with a multifaceted roofline and many fanciful decorative elements. These alterations paralleled the increased prosperity and prominence of its original owner, John McMullen, a successful contractor of the period. *Landmark Number 123*

HAVENS MANSION
AND CARRIAGE HOUSE
1381 South Van Ness Avenue

The Havens Mansion and Carriage House are finely detailed examples of French Second Empire influence on late-nineteenth-century San Francisco residential architecture. Charles Havens, City Architect for twelve years, designed this structure for his personal residence in 1884. In his partnership, Havens and Topke, he designed the San Francisco Yacht Club (1887), the original Mission High School (1909), and the Flatiron Building at 540 Market Street (1913). These buildings reflect the upper-middle-class life-style of San Francisco's "Mansion Row" of the 1880s. *Landmark Number 125*

SHARON BUILDING
Golden Gate Park

The Sharon Building possesses unique historic value. Together with the Carousel and the adjacent Children's Playground, it is the first playground facility built in a public park in the United States. The Sharon Building also acquires architectural significance as a nearly perfect and extremely rare San Francisco example of Victorian Romanesque architecture. This is exemplified by its semicircular arched windows and door openings, squat columns, foliated capitals, contrasting textured stone window trim, stone arabesques, and beautiful rock-faced sandstone wall construction. It was built in 1887 from designs by architects Percy and Hamilton and rebuilt in 1906 and again after a fire in 1980.

The original structure was built with funds bequeathed to the city by William Sharon, "King of the Comstock," an important figure in the early history of San Francisco. *Landmark Number 124*

BRANDENSTEIN HOUSE

(Bransten House)
1735 Franklin Street

The Brandenstein House is a Georgian Style brick structure. Both the architectural style and building material are uncommon in San Francisco domestic architecture. The building reflects the turn-of-the-century national architectural trend away from the forms and extravagances of the Victorian era in favor of more restrained Classical and Colonial Revival forms. The knowledgeable use of architectural detail, well-proportioned massing, and expert placement on the site, all combine to create a design of considerable quality.

The Brandenstein House was built in 1904 by the William Haases from plans by architect Herman Barth. In 1918 the Haases gave it as a wedding present to their daughter Florine on the occasion of her marriage to Edward Bransten (né Brandenstein). William Haas was the first president of the wholesale firm of Haas Brothers, Inc., and Edward Brandenstein's brother Max founded MJB Coffee.

Herman Barth worked as an architect for twenty-five years in San Francisco. Among his designs are the south wing of San Francisco City and County Hospital, the Richmond Masonic Lodge, and the Guggenheim Building at 216–220 Post Street. *Landmark Number 126*

CLUNIE HOUSE
301 Lyon Street

The history of this house, built for Thomas J. Clunie in 1897, reflects San Francisco's changing social scene. Its Victorian elegance survived the earthquake of 1906, two world wars, the hippie era, the drug culture, and consciousness-expanding groups, and it now serves as a bed-and-breakfast.

Architect William Curlett utilized a variety of forms and materials to create an impressive structure for this corner site near the Panhandle of Golden Gate Park. A sophisticated design, the three-layer horizontal composition (concrete base, brick first floor, and frame upper floors) balances the vertical thrust of dormers, chimneys, gables, and a corner bay window capped by a rare open belvedere (one of two remaining in San Francisco).

Thomas Clunie, lawyer, politician, and real-estate speculator, went to considerable expense in building the house, complete with a telephone—rare at the time. When it was constructed, the area was mostly sand dunes. Soon thereafter, the neighborhood became populated with many wealthy and prominent San Franciscans, including both the Spreckles and the Zellerbach families. *Landmark Number 128*

SPAGHETTI FACTORY
478 Green Street

(Not Pictured) Originally a spaghetti factory, this building is an architecturally and visually unremarkable frame structure that was in continuous use from 1908 to 1955, when it was converted to a café and cabaret called The Old Spaghetti Factory. As such, it was an early example of adaptive re-use. The personality of the former proprietor, Frederick Kuh, must be credited with creating the unique character of this establishment. It served as the cultural and social center for San Francisco's bohemians and beatniks and was one of the last gathering spots of its kind in North Beach.

Bohemians and artists gravitated to the North Beach area of San Francisco where the Italian community that inhabited the area had traditionally been sympathetic to artists' needs. A more modern phenomenon seems now to be occurring as venues such as The Old Spaghetti Factory are replaced with a seemingly endless series of trendy restaurants. *Landmark Number 127*

EMPIRE MALT HOUSE

(Bauer & Schweitzer Malting Company)
441–451 Francisco Street

HIBERNIA BANK

1 Jones Street

The Bauer & Schweitzer Malting Company was the last brewing-and-malting operation in North Beach, and the last barrel-malting factory west of the Mississippi. This site has been continuously occupied by brewers and malters since the Lyon Brewery was replaced by the Empire Malt House, operated by John Bauer and Joseph Schweitzer. In 1906, the Empire Malt House was renovated for Bauer & Schweitzer with equipment based upon French designs from the 1860s. Following these renovations, the buildings were almost totally destroyed in 1906. Reconstruction, using reinforced concrete, was completed in 1908. The buildings are now vacant, awaiting a conversion to condominiums. *Landmark Number 129*

The oldest of San Francisco's numerous modified-temple-form banks, Number 1 Jones Street is also one of the best designs for the numerous irregular Market Street intersections. Originally built as a narrow structure along Jones Street in 1892, the building has undergone numerous sympathetic alterations over time, arriving at its present form in 1905. It was rebuilt after the 1906 fire and is one of the city's oldest surviving buildings in the Classical idiom, a style that did not sweep the country until after the Chicago world's fair. The Albert Pissis design is widely admired among architects to this day, although the building currently is vacant and in disrepair. Its most unique architectural features include the domed entrance corner and the fine entrance stairway. It dominates its Market Street corner with unusual authority. *Landmark Number 130*

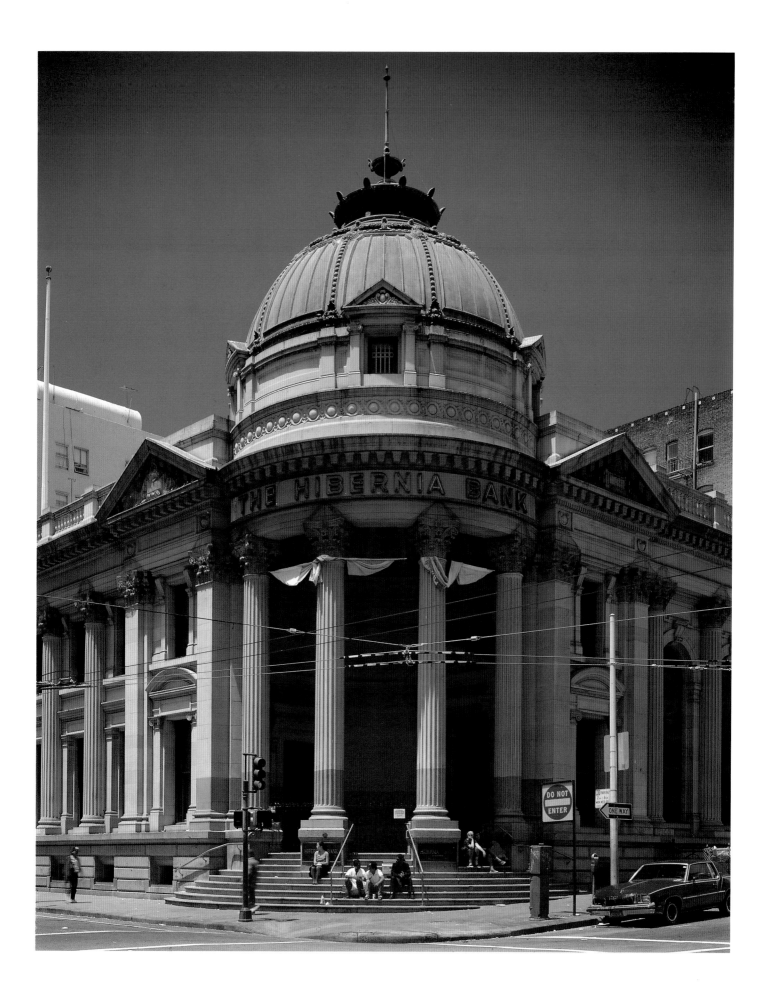

Savings Union Bank

(Cable Car Clothiers) 1 Grant Avenue

The Savings Union Bank of San Francisco is an example of what *Architect and Engineer* called the "first period" of Bliss and Faville's work, characterized by an "enthusiasm for the antique" and influenced by the work of McKim, Mead & White, in whose office both architects had apprenticed. Together with the Union Trust Bank across the street, it forms a gateway to Grant Avenue. The building is a modified temple reputedly derived from the Roman Pantheon. It is a steel-frame structure clad in granite and topped by a reinforced-concrete dome. The main Grant Avenue façade was conceived as a pedimented Ionic temple form featuring a bas-relief of "Liberty" by sculptor Haig Pattigan. The bronze doors (representing the historical succession of the races in the state) and the original interior furnishings were executed by Arthur and Lucia Mathews. *Landmark Number 132*

UNION TRUST BANK

(Branch of the Wells Fargo Bank) 744 Market Street

This was the winning design in a competition for the Union Trust Company (acquired later by the Wells Fargo Bank) by the important architect Clinton Day, who also designed the City of Paris department store. Built in 1910, it is located at an important Market Street intersection across from the Savings Union Bank and the Phelan Building.

The richness of its exterior treatment adds a textural element to the street, suitably enhancing the building's prominence in an area where most of the buildings are less dramatic. The curving Market Street façade seems a perfect solution to the complex intersection. *Landmark Number 131*

AXFORD HOUSE
1190 Noe Street

Recently refurbished, this attractive 1877 Stick Style house-and-carriage-house complex reflects the early rural-scale development of this area of San Francisco. With its garden, iron fence, and hayloft in the gable of the carriage house, this grouping represents one of the earliest developments in the neighborhood. The Axford House originally sported a mansard roof with wrought-iron tracery and its own windmill. *Landmark Number 133*

KERSHAW HOUSE
845 Guerrero Street

Notable for its classic simplicity, broad and well-proportioned cornice, regularly spaced windows with projecting hoods, and wide arched doorway with bracketed porch, this house sits raised above the sidewalk on a landscaped base defined by low walls. It is one of the earliest houses in the Liberty/Hill Historic District and is prominent beyond its size because of its freestanding corner location. *Landmark Number 136*

Potrero School

(Irving M. Scott Primary School) 1060 Tennessee Street

This is the oldest surviving public school in San Francisco and the only one dating back to the nineteenth century. It was founded in 1865 as Potrero School. It moved into new quarters in 1877 on Minnesota near 21st Street (demolished) before the current build-ing, facing Tennessee Street, was added in 1895. The school's name was then changed to honor its benefactor, Irving Murray Scott. The new building was the first school to contain a facility for teaching cooking. *Landmark Number 138*

ST. CHARLES SCHOOL
3250 18th Street

Significant as a rare surviving example of a nineteenth-century schoolhouse, this 1887 building was used for church services until 1894. After that date, the lower floors were converted to classrooms attended by the Sisters of the Holy Cross. The sisters originally consisted of Mother Augusta and seven companions. The school they began at St. Charles grew to an enrollment of four hundred. After 1917, a new church was built on South Van Ness, and the 18th Street building became exclusively a school, a use that has continued to this day. This Italianate structure is one of the very few frame school buildings remaining. *Landmark Number 139*

WESTERFELD HOUSE
1198 Fulton Street

The Westerfeld House is one of the best-known Victorian structures in the West. Its prominent location on Alamo Square near the famous "postcard row" at Steiner and Fulton streets, together with its imposing size, makes it a visitor's delight.

One of the most picturesque examples of the Stick Style Italianate Villa, and one of the largest older buildings in the area, it was designed and built in 1889 by architect Henry Geilfuss as a residence for William Westerfeld, a noted baker and confectioner. An enormous redwood palazzo, it is considered the San Francisco equivalent of Carson House in Eureka, which many call the definitive California Victorian Style residence. Both structures are extremely picturesque versions of the towered villa form, seen here in uncompromising Stick expression with the characteristic squared bays of the 1880s.

Though it is often referred to as the "Russian Consulate," the building's only connection with Russia seems to be that regular meetings of the Russian Club occurred here in the 1940s. Today, after having served variously as a boardinghouse, apartment house, and briefly as a bed-and-breakfast, the Westerfeld House is once again a private residence. *Landmark Number 135*

MECHANICS INSTITUTE
57–65 Post Street

(*Not Pictured*) The 1909 Mechanics Institute building represents one of the earliest educational institutions located at this site (dating from 1866) and is an excellent example of a mixed-use building whose internal functions are expressed in the external design. The ground floor features two retail spaces and a monumental entranceway surmounted by two stories of well-lighted library space, with offices above. The composition is a three-part vertical block with Renaissance/Baroque ornamentation. The marble lobby features an Arthur Mathews mural and a very beautiful circular iron-and-marble stairway. The Mechanics Institute itself occupies three floors, two of them housing the merged Mechanics Institute and Mercantile Libraries. The building is considered a major San Francisco cultural landmark. *Landmark Number 134*

HIGH SCHOOL OF COMMERCE

135 Van Ness Avenue

The High School of Commerce exhibits an exuberant Spanish Colonial Revival design with chiaroscuresque detail. Inspirational sources for the design can be traced specifically to the University of Salamanca in Spain and generally to the increased popularity of Mission and Spanish Colonial Revival stemming from the 1915 Panama-California Exhibition in San Diego. Designed by John Reid, Jr., the building is sheathed in terra-cotta decorated with interspaced diamond-shaped green and pink tiles. The main entrance is flanked with corbels, which are decorated with grotesque figures representing medieval men of learning. The school is built around a central courtyard. In the 1920s, California became noted for its advanced school designs, which often included courtyards or outdoor classroom space that took advantage of the temperate climate.

This school evolved from a commerce department established in the Boy's High School in 1883. The High School of Commerce opened the following year in its own building on Powell Street (near Clay). The school's second building was destroyed in 1906, and a new building was erected on Grove between Polk and Larkin streets. In 1913 this building was moved to 170 Fell Street to make way for the Exposition Auditorium. *Landmark Number 140*

HOME TELEPHONE COMPANY

333 Grant Avenue

This historic building epitomizes a manipulation of Classical vocabulary that is uniquely San Franciscan. The intricate complexities resulting from the exaggerated, overscaled use of the Classical orders juxtaposed against traditionally scaled elements result in an extraordinary and highly successful design. The tripartite composition reflects the various functions of this utility headquarters. The ground floor contained a public lobby (likened to a banking hall) with phone booths for the convenience of subscribers; floors two and three were occupied by administrative offices; and city-wide phone service was provided by the operating exchange on floors four through seven.

Just as the architectural ornamentation is used in an eccentric manner, the history of the building itself is somewhat unique. Home Telephone Company (which built 333 Grant as its central office) figured prominently in the Abraham "Boss" Reuf scandal that rocked City Hall in 1908. The building is also remarkable as a pioneer installation of the telephone-exchange system. *Landmark Number 141*

Notre Dame School
347 Dolores Street

Notre Dame School is a unique and key component of one of San Francisco's most historic areas. The building was designed as a convent and day school for girls. Its imposing mansard-roofed structure of wood and stucco was built in 1907 following the design of an earlier structure on the site, which was dynamited to contain the 1906 fire to the east side of Dolores Street. Elaborate iron gates remain from the previous building. These gates and the garden setting, with its stately palms, reflect the favorable climate that drew the original San Francisco settlers to this spot. *Landmark Number 137*

Pacific Gas & Electric Co., Station J

569 Commercial Street

This structure is a fine example of the high quality of architecture employed by PG&E to beautify its utility stations. The elegant proportions of the building focus attention on the concentrated burst of Renaissance/Baroque ornamentation over the entry. This articulates a sense of "power," which becomes an architectural pun in light of the function for which the building was intended; the pulse generated here spread throughout the surrounding Financial District. When it was converted to a restaurant in the late 1960s, the building provided a different kind of energy to the area. The building now houses offices in a development that extends south to Sacramento Street. *Landmark Number 142*

HOFFMAN GRILL BUILDING
619 Market Street

The smallest remaining building on lower Market Street, 619 Market Street illustrates an architectural restraint and economy of expression typical of postfire construction. Its quality of reserve speaks eloquently of an aesthetic that has virtually vanished from downtown San Francisco. This modest building was designed to complement the hearty, no-nonsense attitude of the establishment it housed, the Hoffman Grill, which operated in this location from 1913. Although the little cigar store that shared the unique set-back entry was absorbed as additional dining space, its odd shape serves as a reminder of an amenity of that period, the after-dinner cigar

that every "good" restaurant had to provide.

The street-level entrance sports its original white porcelain hexagonal tiles, green marble base, and brass railings. The set-back entry also features original dark wood paneling and frosted, beveled glass windows.

The building remained in place while an enormous office tower was built over it. The Planning Commission conditioned approval of the tower on the future occupancy of 619 Market, mandating that it should continue to be used as a period-style restaurant. *Landmark Number 144*

FIREHOUSE, STATION 2
466 Bush Street

The first "thoroughly fireproof structure erected by the City since the fire of 1906," and the first building in San Francisco with Vancouver fine-grain granite facing, this engine house is an example of grand civic architecture on a small scale. It typifies the City Beautiful Movement in relation to a purely utilitarian structure. Prominent Classical features make the station a conspicuous structure, despite its modest size. After a transitional use as a savings-and-loan bank, the building currently houses an art gallery. *Landmark Number 143*

CHRIS' CAFETERIA BUILDING

(Buich Building)
240–242 California Street

Originally Chris' Cafeteria and now the Tadich Grill, this building has long housed important restaurants and retains an interior that dates from the 1920s. Tadich had been in existence since 1865 at two previous locations. It located here in 1965.

One of the finest buildings of its type in the city, in composition it is an enframed window wall with Renaissance/Baroque ornamentation. The handling of materials and colors is superb. Although easily mistaken for copper and bronze, everything but the bronze window frames is actually terra-cotta. The design has been attributed to the firm of Crim and Scott, which also designed a strikingly similar building at 423 Kearny Street in 1909 (now demolished). *Landmark Number 145*

JACK'S RESTAURANT

615 Sacramento Street

This longtime San Francisco restaurant now stands by itself between a large postwar office block and a parking lot. Its composition
is a small, two-part commercial block with a mid-nineteenth-
century upper level that houses private dining rooms. Jack's Edwardian design and ornamentation are reflected by the clinker brick
surrounds, set in stucco walls. *Landmark Number 146*

KERRIGAN HOUSE

(Ruth Cravath Studio, Home, and Stoneyard)

893 Wisconsin Street

(Not Pictured) This building is significant as a San Francisco example
of Bay Area Craftsman bungalow architecture and as the home of
sculptor Ruth Cravath. It is set on a lushly landscaped double lot.
Built in 1905 by Frank W. Kerrigan, a police officer, the property
was the home of Ruth Cravath from 1958 to her death in 1985. She
was active as a sculptor for more than sixty years, and her career
paralleled that of the Bay Area art community for most of this
century. A Chicago native, Cravath served as an art commissioner
and a teacher. A partial list of her commissions includes the Rossi
bust at City Hall, the St. Francis sculpture at Candlestick Park, and
the Thomas Starr King sculpture at the First Unitarian Church.
Landmark Number 148

Dutch Windmill

The Dutch Windmill was constructed to supply water for Golden Gate Park; in 1902, the Park Commission ordered its construction, to the design of Alpheus Bull, Jr. The mill originally pumped 20,000 gallons per hour. In 1913, electric motors were installed to supplement wind power. These motors eventually assumed full pumping capacity and the windmill was left to deteriorate. In 1966, a committee was formed to pursue the restoration of the windmill, which was completed in 1981. *Landmark Number 147*

WILBERT BLACKSMITH SHOP
(Edwin Klockars Blacksmith Shop) 449 Folsom Street

One of the few survivors of the many blacksmiths in this South of Market District in the early twentieth century, this blacksmith shop continues its traditional operation in San Francisco to this day. In this compact wooden building, Edwin Klockars pioneered production of the canning tongs the shop still supplies to canneries across the nation. Pins used to construct one of the bridges across the Willamette River in Portland, elevator track brackets commissioned by Westinghouse for Shasta Dam and Oakland's Kaiser Building, and even fireplace andirons have been hand-wrought at 449 Folsom. Having narrowly avoided replacement by a freeway access ramp, this sturdy frame building endured to exemplify a way of life that has otherwise disappeared from San Francisco. The metal-working shop still produces by hand tools like those offered for sale in catalogues of the original owner, Fred Wilbert, and the business continues to be advertised by a fading painted sign on the east wall. This building is a special and active link with the city's pre-industrial heritage. *Landmark Number 149*

SHEET METAL WORKERS HALL
224–226 Guerrero Street

The San Francisco Sheet Metal Workers Hall is significant as an unusual example of architecture and from its association with the growth of organized labor in San Francisco. The roots of this union reach back to the Iron Cornicemakers Union, Local No. 104, organized in 1886. Original quarters were at Sixth and Market streets, but the building was destroyed by fire in 1906. Temporary quarters at Buchanan and Market streets housed the union until this present building was completed. Dedication ceremonies on December 29, 1906 were attended by 1,200 people, including Mayor Eugene Schmitz and other municipal officers. The structure exhibited the craft of its owners inside and out with an embossed sheet-metal façade, ceilings, and paneling. The hall was used by the union until 1980. It currently serves as living and studio space for artists. *Landmark Number 150*

FLOOD BUILDING

870–898 Market Street

The Flood Building is a monumental Classical Revival pre-earthquake office building, designed by architect Albert Pissis for James Flood, Jr., son of one of the silver kings of Nevada's Comstock Lode. At 12 stories, with 35,000 square feet of space, the Flood Building was the city's largest structure at the time of its construction in 1904. It was originally equipped with steam heat, electric and gas lighting, telephones, and nine elevators. The building burned in 1906, with damage concentrated on the two lower floors. Brick infill in the steel support system is credited with saving the building, although some girders buckled and some sandstone cracked from the heat. Unaltered above the first two floors, the building defines a major Market Street intersection. Its importance is further emphasized by its position as backdrop to the Powell Street cable-car terminus, a popular hub for tourists and residents alike. *Landmark Number 154*

ARCHBISHOP'S MANSION
1000 Fulton Street

This imposing structure was built in 1904 for Archbishop Patrick Riordan, a leader whose devotion to his people and his city formed a legacy still visible in the cultural and physical attributes of San Francisco. When Archbishop Riordan had finished directing the construction of St. Mary's Cathedral, he began work on a residence that would reflect the stateliness of the archdiocese. The resulting Second French Empire Style building is a dignified companion to the Victorian structures that line Alamo Square. The setting, on the northeast corner of the square, is a highly visible element of the Alamo Square Historic District. *Landmark Number 151*

Don Lee Building

1000 Van Ness Avenue

When completed, this building was declared by all who had seen it as the finest automobile-service building in the United States. It was built before a motif for showrooms had evolved. Except for the large ground-floor windows and industrial sash in the upper windows, the structure appears to be an office building or bank; in fact, the smiling California bears on the colonettes had been proposed by the architects on their Bank of Italy design in 1919. Over the doors, the Cadillac corporate heraldry includes two classically languid nudes, a coat of arms, and two 1921 Cadillac wheel options: the eight-spoke traction tire and the twelve-spoke smooth tire. *Landmark Number 152*

EARL C. ANTHONY PACKARD SHOWROOM

(British Motors) 901 Van Ness Avenue

Here is an example of the auto showroom designed as a stage set, where automobiles likened to "magic carpets" were sold to transport people to faraway places. This romantically styled temple, as opulent as the Packards housed within, was a fantasy for those who dreamed of owning a product not yet considered a necessity. Prominent features on the building include twin sets of paired columns at the front corners and a deeply recessed glass-curtain wall. The columns, originally finished to resemble red marble, are topped with elaborate Corinthian capitals. Horizontal elements, such as the frieze and cornice, are light colored and heavily molded with foliate designs. The double-door entrances are articulated by elaborate carved stone moldings. The rear reflects a functional, disciplined design for garage and service. *Landmark Number 153*

FLATIRON BUILDING

540–548 Market Street

The Flatiron Building is one of the few remaining and one of the most distinctive flatirons extant on Market Street. Due to the prevalence of gore blocks north of Market, flatirons were common both before and after the 1906 fire. The subsequent destruction of many such outstanding structures (including the 1892 Crocker Building at Post and Market streets) for high rises and plazas has made the form rare.

Architect Charles Havens's Flatiron Building (backed by the Hobart Building) is made all the more prominent by the adjacent Crown Zellerbach Plaza, while its northern frontage defines the ends of both Sutter and Sansome streets. It contributes strongly to a richly textured and detailed historic enclave around the northern and western sides of Zellerbach Plaza. The skeletal structure of the building is well adapted to a Gothic treatment, unusual for San Francisco, in which tripartite bays are separated by thin piers of reinforced concrete scored to imitate masonry. A highly distinctive cantilevered cornice of Gothic pendants appears to be a prototype for Willis Polk's 1917 Hallidie Building, one block west. Described in 1913 as pure "English Gothic," the medieval ornament is also used for interior railings, grilles, and elevator doors. *Landmark Number 155*

PHELAN BUILDING

760–784 Market Street

This building is the second to occupy this site bearing the name of one of San Francisco's most prominent early families. The first Phelan Building was a six-story, bay-windowed, mansard-roofed flatiron constructed by the elder James Phelan. Destroyed in the fire of 1906, it was quickly replaced by the present building, which, in size alone, justified the 1907 *Call* headline: "Huge Phelan Building Already a Landmark." It was instantly one of the most prominent and important office structures in San Francisco, and in keeping with Phelan's advocacy of the City Beautiful Movement, it greatly dignified both Market Street and the retail district with its two monumental façades. Its prominence was further heightened by the choice of glazed cream terra-cotta; it is probably the largest structure in the city clad with this favorite reconstruction material and an outstanding example of the desire to make of the downtown a "Great White City" like the Chicago world's fair of 1893. *Landmark Number 156*

HILLS BROTHERS COFFEE BUILDING

2 Harrison Street

Established in 1878, Hills Brothers Coffee is the last of the giant coffee firms that originated in San Francisco (others were Folger's, MJB, and Schilling) still located in the city. Founded by Austin and Reuben Hills, the firm began in a stall in the Bay City Market (now United Nations Plaza). In 1882, the firm moved into its first real store. It moved three more times as business expanded—and once due to the 1906 fire—until it located in the present building in 1924.

The Hills Brothers Building was designed by George Kelham, a leading architect in post-1906 San Francisco. The building is in the Romanesque Revival Style, with patterned brickwork, arched doorways and windows, elaborately crafted bronze grillwork doors, and a large tower, which is both functional (gravity aids the blending of coffee beans stored in bins in the tower), as well as ornamental.

A recent addition to the compound includes the large, compatible residential structure pictured in the rendering at right. The architect for the rehabilitation and new construction is the firm of Whistler-Patri. *Landmark Number 157*

Federal Reserve Bank Building

(Law Offices of Orick, Herrington & Sutcliffe) 400 Sansome Street

The 1919 Federal Reserve Bank Building was the first structure built for this system in San Francisco. It is representative of the Federal government's then-growing association with monumental architecture and is an intact contributor to San Francisco's important collection of classically designed banking halls. San Francisco's regional office of the Federal Reserve was first located at 400 Sansome Street. As designed by George Kelham and completed in 1924, the building incorporates the monumental classicism favored by the Federal government and the local tradition of small-scaled banking temples favored by San Francisco's own financial institutions. It is said that the top part of the two-part vertical composition was added as the result of an expanded program after the lower structure was approved.

Following the Federal Reserve relocation to Market Street, the building became an office building for a large law firm. A new east porch replicating the original west colonnade converted the formerly utilitarian rear of the building into a formal addition to the Embarcadero Center complex. *Landmark Number 158*

GAYLORD HOTEL

620 Jones Street

The Gaylord Hotel is a prime example of San Francisco's multiresidential building patterns. Constructed in 1928–29, it was promoted as the "First New York Type Residential Hotel." The structure's design drew on New York–style efficiency-apartment floor plans, with the locally popular Spanish Revival detailing. On the exterior, this ornamentation is evident at the street-level entrance in its glass doors, grillwork, and columns. On the interior, the theme is carried through the quarry-tile flooring, textured plaster walls with ceramic tile inserts, and arched hallways. In the lobby, the original red-and-gold hand-painted wooden ceiling remains intact.

The Gaylord opened with a lavish party attended by local dignitaries on August 7, 1929, but was sold under foreclosure in the 1930s. The current owners are refurbishing the structure with special attention to the original detail. *Landmark Number 159*

ROYAL GLOBE INSURANCE COMPANY BUILDING

201 Sansome Street

One of the richest of all downtown designs in its use of color, materials, and ornamentation, the 1907 Royal Globe Building is located at a major Financial District corner and is an integral part of the Pine and Sansome streetscapes. The building is a three-part vertical composition with eighteenth-century ornament executed in white marble, complemented by red brick, and green-and-white terra-cotta. The base includes an extremely fine carved marble clock over the entrance with a lion and a unicorn. Doors in the elevator lobby are from a seventeenth-century Italian palazzo.

The modern replacement of a heavy upper-level cornice molding with a copper substitute was an ingenious solution worthy of the generation of architects who designed the postfire downtown with less interest in literalness than effect. The patinaed copper recalls the existing green terra-cotta highlights and amplifies the rich play of colors that distinguishes this building. All of the original materials were imported from the East Coast. *Landmark Number 160*

KOHL BUILDING

400 Montgomery Street

The Kohl Building is a handsome and important early San Francisco skyscraper and the only one in the area that survived without any earthquake damage. It was built for Alvinza Hayward. The design was the result of the short-lived association of George W. Percy and Willis Polk, with Henry Meyers as supervising architect. In 1906, the building was burned below the fourth floor and was rebuilt by Polk the next year. In recent years pieces of cornice have been removed.

The Kohl remains an early and excellent example of the more formal decisions that later came to characterize the relatively restrained and correct use of Renaissance/Baroque ornamentation and the two- or three-part compositional formula. It is also an early example of fireproof construction, the success of which can be measured by its unique survival of the fire. *Landmark Number 161*

SHARON BUILDING

39–63 New Montgomery Street

The 1912 Sharon Building is a handsome brick-clad office building with what must be the city's broadest projecting cornice and a narrow L-shaped floor plate that fills the New Montgomery Street and Jesse Alley frontages. It was one of the many buildings constructed for the estate of William Sharon, a colorful pioneer who was a partner in the Palace Hotel and later a United States Senator.

The building is a three-part vertical block composition with Renaissance/Baroque ornamentation and terra-cotta details at the base and capital. It is a "thoroughly fireproof" steel-frame building with reinforced-concrete curtain walls. In both structural system and construction type, this building is considered a model of its day. Appropriately, the original tenants were largely architects or contractors. *Landmark Number 163*

HOBART BUILDING

582–592 Market Street

From just about any point of view, Willis Polk's Hobart Building is one of the most successful tall buildings ever constructed in San Francisco. Located on a mid-block site, it manages to relate to both the diagonal of Market Street in the positioning of the tower and to the north-of-Market grid in the shape of its base. Its glassy commercial base was designed to play the mundane role that should be retained by any street-level space in a commercial area. Its rusticated shaft gives the building an urban character that links it to its neighbors, while its tower gives it a particularly romantic quality that distinguishes it from anything else in San Francisco, or from any other American skyscraper. Its distinctive shape—oval with flat ends—dense terra-cotta ornamental detail, corbeled cornice, and two-leveled tiled hip roof all contribute to its soaring quality. The tower long stood out on the skyline of the city, and although now dwarfed in height, it is still a conspicuous landmark when viewed from Second Street, the location from which it was designed to be seen. It is believed by many to be Polk's finest building. *Landmark Number 162*

McMorry-Lagen House

188–198 Haight Street

(includes Carriage House on Laguna Street)

The McMorry-Lagen House is part of an important Victorian complex significant for its unusually intact interior and exterior detailing. When designated, the interior was a virtual time capsule of the late-nineteenth-century life-style. Only modest adjustments had been made to the systems of the building, such as partial electrification. The upstairs bedrooms retained functional gas lighting, and the kitchen and baths retained their original fixtures (including a copper bathtub). Original carpeting, wallpaper, and custom furniture dating from the time of construction highlight the residence.

The house was built by Farrell McMorry in 1883; his daughter Katie and her husband, Dr. John Lagen, resided in 198 Haight Street, where they raised a family of four. Their daughter, Alice Lagen, inherited the property and at her death the building had been in continuous ownership by the same family for more than one hundred years. *Landmark Number 164*

COIT TOWER
Telegraph Hill Boulevard

Erected with funds from a bequest of Lillie Hitchcock Coit, Coit Tower is a powerful visual landmark, an international symbol of San Francisco, and a reminder of the role Telegraph Hill played in San Francisco's maritime history. An interior elevator provides access to a roof-top viewing deck, which reminds one that historically this site served as a lookout point for spotting vessels arriving through the Golden Gate. The tower is also an example of early, private philanthropic support for civic improvement and beautification in San Francisco and is the site of a recently restored series of important murals executed by a number of noted San Francisco artists. *Landmark Number 165*

TRINITY PRESBYTERIAN CHURCH

3261 23rd Street

This interesting, intact, vernacular Shingle Style structure represents the ecclesiastical architecture of the important architectural firm of Percy and Hamilton. It has a history as a long-term community institution and continues to reflect the changing social complexion of the neighborhood. *Landmark Number 166*

METROPOLITAN LIFE INSURANCE COMPANY BUILDING

(The Ritz-Carlton, San Francisco) 600 Stockton Street

The Metropolitan Life Insurance Company Building is a monumental Classical building, which reflects the style of reconstruction in San Francisco following the 1906 earthquake and fire. In the massive rebuilding of San Francisco in this period, Bay Area architects trained at the Ecole des Beaux-Arts drew upon the revival of Classical forms. This structure, with its many later and compatible additions, is an important example from this significant period of San Francisco's developmental history. It has under gone extensive rehabilitation and is now the Ritz-Carlton, San Francisco, as pictured in this rendering. *Landmark Number 167*

Morgan House

(William Vale House)
2226 California Street

The Frederick Morgan House is significant as an early example of San Francisco Queen Anne Style architecture, designed by noted architect Albert Pissis, in conjunction with Albert Moore. It is also significant as the residence of Frederick Morgan of the Morgan Oyster Company; oystering was an important industry in the Bay Area at the end of the nineteenth century. The building served as the residence of employees of the Mitsui Company until the United States entered World War II. *Landmark Number 168*

GRACE CATHEDRAL CLOSE

1051 Taylor Street

Grace Cathedral is a twentieth-century interpre-
tation of Gothic ecclesiastical architecture executed in steel and reinforced concrete. It is the
third largest Episcopal cathedral in the United
States (behind the Cathedrals of St. John the
Divine in New York and Sts. Peter and Paul in
Washington, D.C.) and the only one with its basic
structure completed. The architect, Lewis
Hobart, was significant in the Bay Area; Ralph
Adam Cram, an architect of national importance, served as consultant. The cathedral house
pictured near the foot of the entrance stair is
scheduled for demolition so that Hobart's grand
stair entrance can be completed. *Landmark
Number 170*

Notre Dame des Victoires Church and Rectory

564–566 Bush Street

Significant as one of San Francisco's early ethnic congregations, Notre Dame des Victoires has been known as the "French Church" since 1856, when Gustav Touchard purchased the site from a Baptist congregation. In 1885, Archbishop Riordan gave the church to the Marist Fathers. The 1906 earthquake and fire destroyed the church structure, which was then rebuilt by the congregation on the same site. It is a replica of a Catholic church in Lyon, France. The current structure features a base with double stairways leading to a foyer with stained-glass windows beneath a semicircular apse, which is, in turn, positioned between twin towers topped by open belvederes. The adjacent rectory exhibits a rusticated base, a smooth-finished midsection with arched window openings, and a dormered tile roof. The centennial of the founding of the church was commemorated by a plaque given by the Republic of France in 1956. *Landmark Number 173*

CAMPFIRE GIRLS BUILDING

(San Francisco Jewish Community Center,
Rothenberg Early Childhood Center)
325 Arguello Street

Originally built as the Campfire Girls Building, this is a beautiful
and picturesque example of Bay Area Craftsman Style architecture.
Its interior features reflect the quality of the design: redwood was
used for trim, paneling, and beams in the trussed cathedral vaults of
the Great Hall. It was built in 1929 to the designs of architect Henry
Gutterson. *Landmark Number 169*

REFUGEE SHACK

1227 24th Avenue

This little house is a reminder of San Francisco's unique municipal rehousing program that followed the devastation of the 1906 earthquake and fire. That natural disaster left thousands homeless, many of whom had few resources with which to reconstruct a home. Temporarily housed in army-issue tents immediately following the April disaster, the homeless needed more substantial shelter to endure the winter season, and 5,610 of these simple wooden cottages were erected, leased to the homeless, and eventually purchased and moved to privately owned lots. By the summer of 1908, public lands were cleared of the temporary settlements and the little houses (average size of 10 by 14 feet) were scattered throughout the city. Like this one, most were augmented with porches and other additions over time. Approximately twenty still exist in San Francisco. *Landmark Number 171*

PARK SUPERINTENDENT'S RESIDENCE

(McLaren Lodge)
John F. Kennedy Drive
Golden Gate Park

The Mediterranean Style McLaren Lodge was built in 1896 and is located near the entrance to Golden Gate Park. It originally served as the official residence of the Park Superintendent, the second of whom was Scotsman John McLaren, who held that position (and resided in the building) for fifty-three years. McLaren gained international attention for his work in the 1915 Panama-Pacific International Exposition.

The structure now houses the offices of the Recreation and Park Department. A large evergreen in front of the lodge is lighted every year and serves, unofficially, as San Francisco's public holiday tree. *Landmark Number 175*

St. Boniface Church and Rectory

133 Golden Gate Avenue

St. Boniface Church, operated by the Franciscan Fathers since 1887, is the oldest German Catholic church in San Francisco. It was established in 1860 with antecedents reaching back to 1852. The church has long been a mainstay of San Francisco's large German community and today serves as a reminder of that community's former prominence in the downtown. The present Romanesque Revival building is a reconstruction of its predecessor and was erected following the earthquake and fire of 1906. With its imposing three-part composition and its tall tower, it has long been a visual landmark in the Tenderloin District. It contains an extremely fine and richly detailed interior, which has been recently restored. *Landmark Number 172*

SPRECKLES CAR HOUSE

(Geneva Car Barn)

2301 San Jose Avenue

The Spreckles Car House is the last original car house of San Francisco's street-railway system. Built in 1899 by John D. Spreckles of the sugar-refining fortune, the complex served San Francisco's first electric train line and the only interurban line (it provided service to San Mateo on the Peninsula). San Francisco's street-railway system opened up the city's outlying areas for development. The complex housed San Francisco's historic private cars during operation of the Market Street Railway Company (1921–44). The car house has continued in use under the Municipal Railway System, with recent renovations to the yard to accommodate light-rail vehicles. Though the building is currently vacant and damaged by the 1989 earthquake, the city continues to search for ways to reuse it. *Landmark Number 180*

THEODORE GREEN
APOTHECARY

500 Divisadero Street

The Theodore Green Apothecary, built in 1888, is a rare San
Francisco example of the work of noted architect Samuel Newsom.
It is also the site of a long-term neighborhood commercial establishment and is a rare surviving example of an intact nineteenth-
century storefront. *Landmark Number 182*

Das Deutsches Haus

(California Hall)

625 Polk Street

California Hall is a finely detailed example of the German Renaissance architectural style, rarely seen in San Francisco. Constructed in 1912 from funds raised by German societies, the building, originally called Das Deutsches Haus, served as a social center for the German community. The cornerstone was laid by John Hermann, founder of the Hermann Safe Company, which remains in business today. The hall opened with an elaborate celebration that included a message of personal best wishes from Kaiser Wilhelm. The design of the structure is said to be reminiscent of Heidelberg Castle in Germany. By the late 1970s, the building had fallen into decline and was the location of a scandalous police-cadet party before it was purchased and restored by its current owner. It now serves as a home for the California Culinary Academy. *Landmark Number 174*

CROWN ZELLERBACH COMPLEX AND SITE

1 Bush Street

The Crown Zellerbach Complex is significant for its association with a prominent San Francisco family and corporation, for its design by a noted architectural firm that has shaped building trends in this century, and for its aesthetically attractive open space.

Anthony Zellerbach came to California during the Gold Rush, and to San Francisco in 1868. In 1870 he established a small stationery business not far from the site of the current Crown Zellerbach building. The business grew into a paper-products enterprise now deeply rooted in the economic life of the United States and Canada. His grandson, James David ("J.D.") worked in the family business at all levels and ultimately became chairman of the board. He was a socially prominent and civic-minded San Franciscan, and his concerns for the revitalization of the city found expression in the Blyth-Zellerbach Committee of 1955, which funded site plans for San Francisco's first redevelopment project: the Golden Gateway.

The San Francisco offices of Skidmore, Owings & Merrill (which opened in 1946) and Hertzka and Knowles were selected by Zellerbach to design a new headquarters for the family company. San Francisco had witnessed the construction of only one high rise (the Equitable Building) since 1930. The Crown Zellerbach Building, with its radical, elegant design and environmental departure from the city's past marked the beginning of the most sweeping revitalization seen since 1906. The resulting skyline is largely dominated by the works of Skidmore, Owings & Merrill.

Architectural critics Sally and John Woodbridge describe the complex as "the first of the city's glass-curtain–walled towers in the first and the best of the tower-plaza settings. [The] expensive walls of the tower, where the air-conditioning console is set in to permit the glass to extend unbroken from the floor to above the ceiling, will never be done again. The same goes for the elegant but extravagant placement of the stairs in their own mosaic-clad tower, outside the office block. The playful form of the round retail building is an integral part of the plaza composition." *Landmark Number 183*

CADILLAC HOTEL
366–394 Eddy Street

The Cadillac Hotel is a noteworthy example of the work of the important architectural firm of Meyer and O'Brien. From 1902 to 1908 Frederick Meyer and Smith O'Brien were partners, producing some of the city's finest buildings. The triple-bay design of the hotel is unusual in apartment-hotel construction. The building of the Cadillac Hotel in 1908 foreshadowed the development of the Tenderloin District as a major residential neighborhood, which was subsequently stimulated by the 1915 Panama-Pacific International Exposition.

The Cadillac Hotel was also the former home of the oldest professional boxing establishment in the United States, Newman's Gym, which was located in a street-level retail space in the hotel structure. From 1924 to 1984, Newman's hosted nearly all the great names of professional boxing. *Landmark Number 176*

First Congregational Church

432 Mason Street

The First Congregational Church is an excellent example of the work of the Reid Brothers, a prominent architectural firm whose work influenced the development of the city. The building serves as an example of the then-innovative construction technique of reinforcing concrete with steel bars, which became very popular during the post-1906 reconstruction period and continues in limited use to this day. The church also serves to reflect the role in social history played by this denomination: the building's use of the Classical Revival Style, which is most frequently seen in San Francisco's banking temples, suggests the desire of the church to remain in, and be a part of, the business character of the downtown. *Landmark Number 177*

LAWN BOWLING
CLUBHOUSE AND GREENS
Golden Gate Park

The Lawn Bowling Clubhouse and Greens are among the earliest
remaining examples of organized recreational activities in Golden
Gate Park. Formed in 1901, the Lawn Bowling Club constructed its
clubhouse in 1915 during John McLaren's tenure as Park Superintendent. The clubhouse's restrained Edwardian architecture is
somewhat prosaic, but when viewed with the white-clad membership on the lush green lawn, the complex takes on the dreamlike
quality of another time. *Landmark Number 181*

Turn Hall
(The Women's Building)
3543 18th Street

Through its name changes over time, this exceptional Mission Revival building reflects the character of its evolving neighborhood. It was built as Turn Hall in 1910. It was an outgrowth of the German turnverein movement—the name translates literally as "exercise club," and the building housed gymnastics equipment for its members. This "sound body, sound mind" philosophy spawned turnvereins throughout the country and developed a normal-school curriculum that trained gymnastics instructors. This movement was instrumental in introducing physical education into the American public-school system.

In 1935 the building became Dovre Hall, reflecting social changes in the Mission District community. The hall was leased by Norwegian immigrants and renamed after their legendary Dovre Mountains: "united and true until Dovre may fall." The building was remodeled as a social club, with the gymnasium being replaced by a dance hall, complete with a stage and refreshment concession. Over the next several decades, the building was used as a meeting hall for many social institutions.

In 1978, as a result of the growth of the women's movement, the building was sold to the San Francisco Women's Centers, which continues the tradition of using this building as a gathering place for the contemporary social and political clubs of the Mission District. *Landmark Number 178*

Beach Chalet
1000 The Great Highway

The 1925 Beach Chalet is noted for its design by the legendary early San Francisco architect Willis Polk, its location in Golden Gate Park, and its important interior frescoes, executed by French artist Lucien Labault, who immigrated to San Francisco in 1910. The building was constructed as a municipal restaurant and pavilion along the Ocean Beach frontage of the park. The interior artwork was done later with funding provided by the WPA Federal Art Project as part of President Roosevelt's New Deal economic-recovery program. The now-vacant city-owned building and its murals have been recently restored. *Landmark Number 179*

MARK HOPKINS HOTEL
1 Nob Hill / 850 Mason Street

The 1923 Mark Hopkins Hotel, designed by the architectural firm of Weeks and Day, is best known for the sweeping views from its top-floor cocktail lounge. The Top of the Mark (original interior design by Miller and Pflueger) is the most famous lounge in San Francisco and a forerunner of all hotel-top restaurant-and-view lounges. This site was originally the location of the most elaborate of the Nob Hill residences, the home of magnate Mark Hopkins. The granite retaining walls, built in 1875, which support the perimeter of the site, remain intact. The hotel was the site of meetings concerning the founding of the United Nations and was subsequently used for U.N. Charter meetings in 1945. It is one of San Francisco's grand hotels and social and cultural centers. *Landmark Number 184*

LEWIS HOUSE
4143 23rd Street

FIREHOUSE,
ENGINE COMPANY No. 37
2501 25th Street

(Not Pictured) This 1892 Queen Anne Style structure is an example of working-class row houses of the nineteenth century. Its original owner, David Lewis, was a partner in the cabinet-and-stair-building firm of Vandenburgh and Lewis. Its exterior design combines rustic siding on the first floor with alternating bands of fish-scale and diamond-pattern shingles on the second floor, gable, and corner tower. The interior features original custom-built cabinetry, bookcases, and built-in desks. *Landmark Number 186*

This firehouse is architecturally significant as an example of early-twentieth-century municipal commitment to high-quality design in public buildings. The structure is part of a city institution whose great importance lies in the community memory of the destruction of the 1906 earthquake and fire. The building was designed by Clarence Ward and completed in 1918; its front elevation is formed from a central section with seven terra-cotta–framed windows flanked by a pedimented wing on each end. *Landmark Number 187*

FIREHOUSE, ENGINE COMPANY No. 8

1648 Pacific Avenue

The original firehouse on this site was destroyed in 1906. A temporary structure served until this building was completed in 1917. It functioned until 1980, when it was closed and declared surplus city property. Its handsome brick-and-terra-cotta façade is typical of the high-quality design of public buildings of this period. This Pacific Avenue firehouse was designed by City Architect John Reid, Jr. *Landmark Number 188*

FAIRMONT HOTEL

590 Mason Street

Designed by San Francisco's Reid Brothers, the
1902–6 Fairmont Hotel, with its richly detailed
exterior, elegant porte cochere, and opulent lobby
reflects the finest tradition of Nob Hill "society"
architecture. The Fairmont is the grandest of San
Francisco's grand hotels and even today draws
celebrity guests from the worlds of entertainment,
sports, and politics. Like that of the Mark Hopkins, this site was originally occupied by a residence; in this case it was owned by James Fair, a
Comstock silver king. Until recently, the Fairmont was used for location photography as the
fictitious St. Gregory Hotel on the television
series *Hotel*. *Landmark Number 185*

SOUTHERN PACIFIC COMPANY HOSPITAL COMPLEX

1400 Fell Street, 1555 and 1559 Hayes Street

Constructed from 1907 to 1911 to the designs of Southern Pacific in-house architect Daniel J. Patterson, this is the oldest intact hospital complex in the city. Covering a full city block, the complex comprises five freestanding structures: the hospital building, nurses' annex, Huntington Social Hall, powerhouse, and paint shop. All of these structures exhibit a high quality of monumental Neoclassical design, including the surrounding decorative metal fence supported by piers that match those of the masonry buildings. *Landmark Number 191*

EDWARDS HOUSE

1366 Guerrero Street

The Frank G. Edwards House, constructed in 1883, is a noteworthy example of transitional flat-front Italianate design. Edwards was an importer, publisher, and civic leader who made significant contributions to the development of the city. Located on a 50-by-125-foot lot, the Edwards House continues to convey the larger parcel pattern of development that existed in the nineteenth century. *Landmark Number 189*

Oakley Residence and Flats

200–202 Fair Oaks Street

Pacific Hardware and Steel Company

(Baker and Hamilton Building)
700 Seventh Street

(Not Pictured) Constructed in 1886 for contractor William Oakley and his wife, Jenny, a dressmaker, this two-story (over basement) Stick Style building visually dominates its setting, due to the unusual richness of its architectural detailing. *Landmark Number 192*

Designed by the San Francisco architectural firm of Sutton and Weeks, 700 Seventh Street is a three-story masonry warehouse and office structure, typical of American industrial buildings of the early twentieth century. The building initiated the development of its neighborhood as a manufacturing and warehouse district. *Landmark Number 193*

THIRD STREET BRIDGE
(Francis "Lefty" O'Doul Bridge)
Third near Berry Street

This is a unique modern drawbridge, designed and patented by J. B. Strauss, the engineer who designed the Golden Gate Bridge. It is the only one of its type in the Bay Area. The main span consists of a 143-foot-long, riveted-steel, single-leaf bascule truss, complete with electrically driven hoist. The south approach span consists of four 23-foot concrete girders; the north end is a 54-foot-long riveted-steel girder. The entire structure rests on a concrete substructure supported on driven timber piles. The two small harbormaster's cottages are original. *Landmark Number 194*

HINKEL HOUSE AND CARRIAGE HOUSE

280 Divisadero Street

Constructed in 1885 as the residence of Charles L. Hinkel, 280 Divisadero Street is an unusual example of transitional Second French Empire residential architecture. Hinkel was a member of a prominent family of developers and builders who, over four generations, contributed significantly to the residential development of San Francisco. Hinkel reserved a large lot for his residence and built a quality structure with elaborate detailing on all exterior walls. Most buildings of the period had plain side and rear walls with the Victorian detailing reserved for only the front elevation. The Hinkel residence sported lavish interior furnishings, substantial landscaping, and its own carriage house. *Landmark Number 190*

ISLAM TEMPLE
650 Geary Street

One of San Francisco's most unusual buildings, this elaborately eclectic fantasy, designed by well-known Scottish architect (and Shriner) T. Patterson Ross and influenced by the Alhambra in Granada, Spain, reflects the cultural interests of the Shriners, for whom it was designed. It displays the Moorish motifs used in their ceremonies and was declared one of the finest Shrine temples in America when it was completed in 1918. The façade, with its Byzantine arches and filigree latticework, is constructed of ornate polychrome terra-cotta with a granite base. The ground floor provides the main entrance to the meeting hall and entrances to subgrade commercial parking with neon signage. *Landmark Number 195*

HANSON HOUSE
126 27th Avenue

(*Not Pictured*) The 1907 Hanson residence is one of the oldest structures in the Middle Richmond District. Its picturesque variation of Shingle Style design with flared-tip gables is the work of architect Charles Flugger. *Landmark Number 197*

SPRECKLES MANSION
2080 Washington Street

One of the best-known private residences in the city, largely because of its elaborate French Baroque limestone façade, sweeping grounds, and prominent siting, this mansion is often referred to as the Sugar Palace, a reference to the Spreckles's sugar fortune. The owners, Adolph and Alma Spreckles, were known for their art patronage: they donated the Palace of the Legion of Honor to the city. It was designed by architect George Applegarth who also designed their home, which was built in 1912. *Landmark Number 196*

QUEEN HOUSE
2212 Sacramento Street

(Not Pictured) This is the only remaining intact residence in San Francisco designed by A. Page Brown, who was considered to be one of the city's most important turn-of-the-century architects. Though he was better known for his nonresidential work, particularly the Ferry Building (Landmark No. 90) and Trinity Church (Landmark No. 16), Brown actually produced more homes than commercial structures. Most of these homes were built in Oakland and Hillsborough in the Bay Area, and Santa Barbara in southern California. Brown died in a riding accident before the Queen House was completed. The *San Francisco Chronicle* of December 4, 1896 credits the completion of the house to Frank S. Van Trees, who worked in Brown's office and was also the architect for the Koshland House (Landmark No. 95). *Landmark Number 198*

APPENDIX I: HISTORIC DISTRICTS

THE CITY AND COUNTY OF SAN FRANCISCO

N

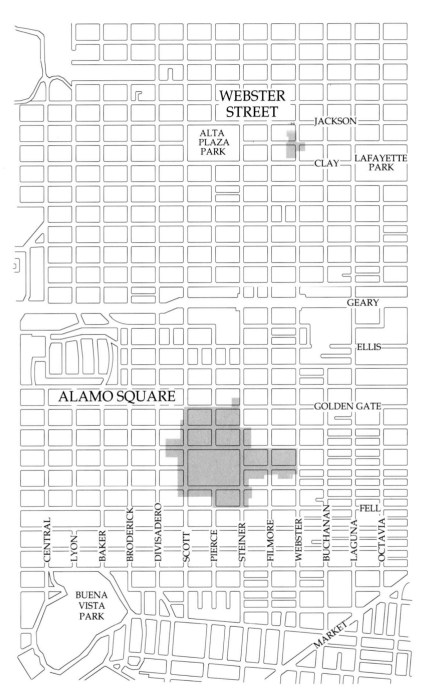

WEBSTER STREET
STREET
JACKSON
ALTA
PLAZA
PARK
CLAY LAFAYETTE
PARK

GEARY

ELLIS

ALAMO SQUARE

GOLDEN GATE

FELL

CENTRAL
LYON
BAKER
BRODERICK
DIVISADERO
SCOTT
PIERCE
STEINER
FILMORE
WEBSTER
BUCHANAN
LAGUNA
OCTAVIA

BUENA
VISTA
PARK

MARKET

WEBSTER STREET HISTORIC DISTRICT
(25 properties)

This Historic District consists almost entirely of residences built in 1878–80 in the Italianate Style. It has a common scale, nearly uniform height, setbacks, and vertical emphasis. The architectural consistency is remarkable and worth preserving. Most of the houses have retained their original detailing while others have had the details restored.

The builders of the district include the Real Estate Associates who constructed six houses in the district and nearly one thousand citywide, two hundred of which remain.

The district represents typical middle-class residential living of its period. It is not a museum, however, but a group of comfortable, practical homes for people of today. Economically, it has proven its vigor by continuing to be in residential use. Its visual appeal is readily apparent and photographs of Webster Street often appear in print.

ALAMO SQUARE HISTORIC DISTRICT
(276 properties)

The Alamo Square Historic District is significant as a continuum of residential design by distinguished architects spanning the period from the 1870s to the 1920s. The towered Westerfeld House on Fulton Street and the renowned Steiner Street "Postcard Row"—so called because of its popularity as a best-selling postcard image, with its Victorian foreground and downtown-skyline background—are as closely identified the world over with San Francisco as are the cable cars and Coit Tower. The district is unified in its residential character and relatively small scale, as well as construction type, materials, ornamentation, and basements and retaining walls used to adjust for the often steep hillside sites. Included within the boundaries are the Alamo Square Park, its edges, and most of the nearby buildings, all equally distinguished. The district serves as a visual reminder of how past generations lived.

Chinatown Historic District [Proposed]
(353 properties)

San Francisco's Landmarks Board signaled its intent to preserve Chinatown's buildings on October 16, 1985. Since that time, numerous public hearings and many public debates over this national treasure have ensued. The opposition seems to fear that the designation would prohibit necessary structural improvements, institutionalize the existing overcrowded conditions, and thwart potential development. While none of this would necessarily happen, even the possibility that it might has been sufficient to stall the proposed designation. After six years, the district has still not had a hearing at the Planning Commission. It is included here because without it no book on San Francisco landmarks could be considered complete.

San Francisco's Chinatown has been a favorite tourist destination for over 140 years. Visitors find it difficult to resist Chinatown's color, scale, and atmosphere. The opportunity for distinctive educational, shopping, and dining experiences are equally inviting. The major thoroughfare, Grant Avenue, is lined with an exceptional mix of shops and boutiques, arts-and-crafts bazaars, and cafés. The side streets offer a glimpse into San Francisco's past that exists in no other part of the city.

Chinatown has been a haven for the Chinese since about 1850; its celebrity derives from this ethnic heritage and the fact that it is the oldest section of San Francisco. The District is unique in its ability to retain a village-like charm while surrounded by high rises and to serve a population that is among the most dense in America.

Following the earthquake of 1906, Chinatown was rebuilt with a significant concentration of Chinese-style architectural elements overlaying what is essentially a group of Edwardian-style buildings. While much of this sinocized architecture was built to promote goodwill between the two communities, much of it was clearly a private expression of Chinese culture, housing the temples and family associations within the neighborhood and not intended for tourists.

What was sensationalized in the nineteenth century as a ghetto of racial peculiarity and cultural oddity is admired today as an ethnic neighborhood where cultural traditions are preserved. This image of Chinatown as an unassimilated foreign enclave remains unchanged. The significance of Chinatown as a Historic District lies not in cultural exotics, but in its intrinsic historic value: no other San Francisco neighborhood contains such a concentration of landmarks dating to or associated with the Gold Rush. Its presence is a continuing reminder of the progress of the Chinese in America and consequently reflects an important part of the political past of the city, state, and nation. As such, it is a unique American entity of international significance.

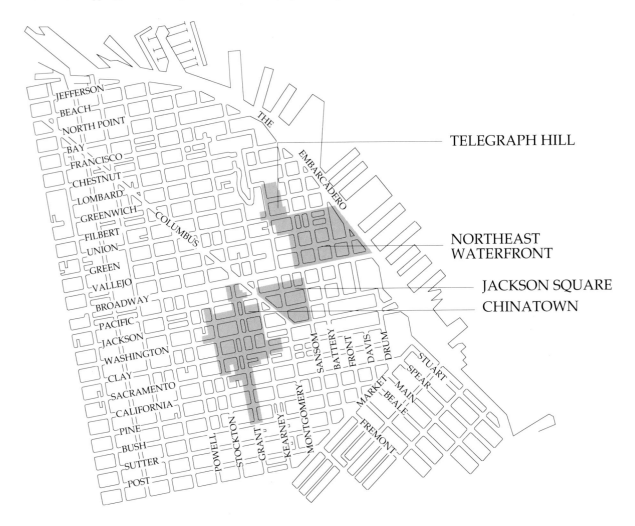

NORTHEAST WATERFRONT HISTORIC DISTRICT
(51 properties)

The Northeast Waterfront Historic District contains commercial warehouse buildings from nearly every decade of San Francisco's history. The area reflects the waterfront storage and maritime activities that were an important aspect of San Francisco's business history. These buildings range in age from the early clipper-ship warehouses of Scotsman Daniel Gibb in the 1850s to the properties owned by the General Engineering and Drydock Company of the 1940s, a company crucial to the shipbuilding effort that made the San Francisco Bay Area the major Pacific maritime support facility during World War II.

The original shoreline of Yerba Buena swept in a curve from Montgomery Street to roughly Jackson Street and on to the deep water slightly east of Battery Street. The first Pacific Mail steamer to arrive in San Francisco unloaded passengers in this area in 1848, and the unique clipper ships built expressly for San Francisco's Gold Rush trade docked in this area.

During the Gold Rush era, the boundaries of the area were extended eastward by landfill into the Bay in order to create new warehouse space. Large sections of Telegraph Hill were excavated for the fill. In the late 1880s a seawall was built that established the eastern boundary of the area. A number of ships are presumed to have been buried beneath the fill used to extend the district. A ship buried in 1851 as an extension of Frederick Griffing's wharf was recently unearthed during the excavation of Levi Plaza along the northern boundary of the district.

These warehouse facilities were in continuous use from the Gold Rush to the 1960s. Since that time, many of them have been converted to showrooms, offices, and retail establishments. Since warehouse architecture did not undergo profound stylistic changes until the introduction of reinforced concrete, the structures built both before and after the fire embody the original appearance and spirit of the area. Of particular note is the block bounded by Front, Battery, Union, and Green streets, the most cohesive extant brick-warehouse complex from this era in the city. In addition, cobblestone paving and the narrow-gauge belt-line railroad tracks that served the district are visible at the foot of Commerce Street. The area serves as a visual reminder of San Francisco's earlier maritime and warehousing activity.

JACKSON SQUARE HISTORIC DISTRICT
(84 properties)

Jackson Square contains virtually all of the city's surviving commercial buildings from the 1850s and 60s. This area, close to Portsmouth Plaza, where the major segment of the modern city began, was the central business district of those early times. Its waterfront location led to its mercantile and financial character, but the district also contained consulates and offices. Many distinguished men had businesses or property in the area, including William Tecumseh Sherman, Colonel Jonathan Stevenson, Mayors Charles Brenham and Ephraim Burr, Domingo Ghirardelli, Anson Hotaling, Faxton Dean Atherton, William Lent, Alexander Grogan, and James Fremery. The original waterline came to Montgomery and Jackson streets, and the present district is partly on filled ground. Some of the landfill consists of the hulls of ships abandoned in the rush to the gold fields.

More than any other existing part of San Francisco, this area recalls the gold-and-silver era and the days of the Vigilante Movement.

The Barbary Coast, north of the original commercial area, had a somewhat different but noteworthy history. Although the present buildings do not date from the nineteenth century, many of them were built immediately after the 1906 earthquake and fire and embody the spirit and appearance of the earlier city. In fact, ever since the 1850s this area to the south of Telegraph Hill has had a bawdy reputation.

TELEGRAPH HILL HISTORIC DISTRICT
(94 properties)

Telegraph Hill is one of the world's most famous hills. Its landmass has been a visual landmark to sailors entering the Bay since its discovery by Captain Juan Manuel de Ayala on August 5, 1775. It is known as "the hill that's been around the world" because great portions of it were blasted out for ballast used in sailing ships. At the ship's destination, the ballast was put ashore (and often used as paving material) and replaced by new cargo bound for California. The hill's current configuration is the result of quarrying. The rock was also used to build Gold Rush era warehouses, to fill the flatlands east of the hill, and to build the seawall that stabilized San Francisco's waterfront. The last quarrying took place in 1914.

This Historic District is a unique expression of the pattern of development that took place on the eastern slope of Telegraph Hill from 1850 to 1939. Topographic constraints shaped the original settlement of the hill. The difficulty of access on the hillsides and cliffs and proximity to the waterfront area first produced a community of waterfront workers housed in cloth-lined shacks and modest houses. Intact groupings of these buildings remain within the district and make up the city's largest concentration of pre-1870 frame structures. The Napier Lane houses represent an especially intact group of surviving structures from the mid-nineteenth century.

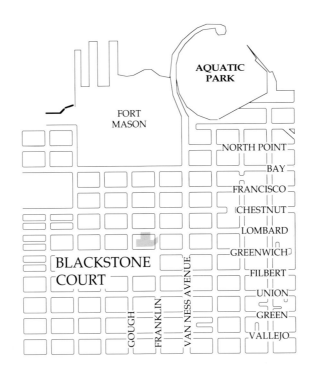

AQUATIC PARK

FORT MASON

NORTH POINT
BAY
FRANCISCO
CHESTNUT
LOMBARD
GREENWICH
FILBERT
UNION
GREEN
VALLEJO

BLACKSTONE COURT

GOUGH
FRANKLIN
VAN NESS AVENUE

BUSH
SUTTER
POST
GEARY
O'FARRELL
ELLIS
EDDY
TURK
GOLDEN GATE

VAN NESS
HYDE
LEAVENWORTH
JONES
TAYLOR
MASON

BEALE
FIRST
SECOND
THIRD

MARKET
MISSION
HOWARD
FOLSOM
HARRISON
BRYANT
BRANNAN
TOWNSEND

FOURTH
FIFTH

EIGHTH
NINTH

HAYES
FELL

CIVIC CENTER

SOUTH END

CHINA BASIN

BLACKSTONE COURT HISTORIC DISTRICT
(5 properties)

The significance of Blackstone Court is primarily historic. It is essentially an enclave of five structures, one of which, Blackstone House, though considerably altered, is thought to be historically important. The house is located off a blind alley, the north line of which recalls an early trail—shown on 1850s U.S. Coast Survey maps—that led to the Presidio. An early plant nursery was established here in 1885 and lasted until 1947.

Occasionally, the landmarking process is used for planning considerations that do not really involve historic preservation. An example of this is when a designation is sought primarily to obtain an official decision against further development. Such may be the case with the Blackstone Court Historic District: at this writing, the Landmarks Board has voted to rescind its designation.

SOUTH END HISTORIC DISTRICT
(73 properties)

For decades after the Gold Rush, San Francisco was the principal West Coast seaport. San Francisco's expansion and transformation into one of the most important cities in North America is attributable to the location of its deep-water port. Inland valleys beyond the coastal mountain range were accessible by an extensive system of rivers and canals, unique to the Pacific Coast. The size, shelter, deep water, and location of the harbor made San Francisco a gateway to foreign lands as well as to fertile interior valleys.

The warehouses developed over a sixty-year period along the southern waterfront provide a view of architectural and technological responses to the rapid changes of a growing industrial nation, state, and city, and the interdependence of architecture and history can be traced from the evolution of those warehouses. Like its counterpart in the Northeast Waterfront Historic District, the South End contains an extraordinary concentration of buildings from almost every period of San Francisco's maritime history.

This rich diversity and concentration of architectural forms provides the greatest rationale for the protection offered by designation. The maritime activities served by these warehouses were some of the most important, economically and socially, in the development of the city, and they provided inspiration to industrialists, merchants, unionists, immigrants, and artists.

CIVIC CENTER HISTORIC DISTRICT [PROPOSED]
(42 properties)

San Francisco's Civic Center is recognized for its significance in architecture and history. Nominated in 1988, this proposed Historic District awaits final confirmation by the Board of Supervisors and the Mayor.

The land on which the Civic Center stands was declared a City Hall Reservation as early as 1870. In 1904, Mayor Phelan led the formation of the Association for the Improvement and Adornment of San Francisco. They invited Daniel Burnham to prepare a grand plan for the city, with B. J. S. Cahill providing a design for the Civic Center. Following the 1906 earthquake, the public wanted an expedient plan for the reconstruction of city-government offices, and a modified version of the Cahill Plan was approved by the Board of Supervisors in 1909.

The Civic Center development effort, spearheaded by Mayor Rolph and encouraged by the imminent 1915 Panama-Pacific International Exposition, saw the Civic Center as the permanent expression of the city's grandeur and vitality, which the exposition would exemplify on a temporary basis.

The Exposition Auditorium, the Central Plaza, the Powerhouse, and the new City Hall were completed by late 1915 in time to impress visitors drawn to the exposition. The Library was completed in 1916, the State Building in the 1920s, and the Public Health and Federal buildings in the 1930s, when the Opera House and the Veteran's Building were also finished. The original Plaza was replaced in the 1950s with an underground garage.

The design of the Civic Center was the city's architectural expression of its new international importance. At the time it was taking form, geography and historical events had made San Francisco the most prominent city in the West, and monumental Classical architecture for its central public space embodied this consciousness and the accompanying belief that such inspiring surroundings should be democratically available to all.

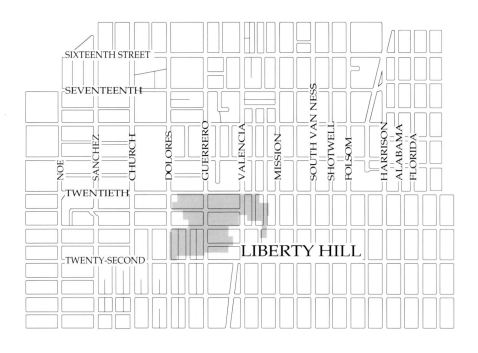

SIXTEENTH STREET
SEVENTEENTH
NOE
SANCHEZ
CHURCH
DOLORES
GUERRERO
VALENCIA
MISSION
SOUTH VAN NESS
SHOTWELL
FOLSOM
HARRISON
ALABAMA
FLORIDA
TWENTIETH
TWENTY-SECOND
LIBERTY HILL

LIBERTY / HILL HISTORIC DISTRICT
(293 properties)

Taking its name from Liberty Street and Hill Street, the Liberty/Hill Historic District is significant in its intact representation of nineteenth-century middle-class housing and development practices. It is one of the earliest residential suburbs to be developed in San Francisco, with major building starting in the 1860s and continuing until the turn of the century. Since the fire that followed the 1906 earthquake was stopped at the 20th Street boundary of the district, examples of all architectural styles prevalent during the development period are represented.

The district's houses range in size from the small workingmen's cottages on Lexington and San Carlos Streets, with their uniform façades and setbacks, to the custom-built houses found on Liberty or Fair Oaks streets. While there were only a few grand houses in the district, a number were designed by architects well known in the Bay Area, including Albert Pissis, the Newsom brothers, William H. Topke, Charles Havens, and Charles J. Rousseau.

The suburban quality of the Liberty/Hill area is retained to this day. It is enhanced by extensive street tree plantings and the low incidence of commercial establishments. The majority of the district's businesses are on Valencia Street, a historic and unifying commercial corridor. Seventy percent of the buildings are Victorian in style; nearly one-third are architect designed.

APPENDIX II: DESIGNATED STRUCTURES OF MERIT

The purpose of this list is to recognize and encourage the protection, enhancement, perpetuation, and use of these structures without placing any specific restriction on them. This designation usually has been used for buildings that lack sufficient architectural integrity, due to extensive alteration. The lack of activity in the category is reflected in the numbering system wherein the first two numbers refer to the year of the designation, and the number after the decimal indicates the number of such cases designated that year.

CM 67.1   The Murphy Windmill
           Golden Gate Park

CM 68.1   The Cannery
           2801 Leavenworth

CM 69.1   One Jackson Place
           Enter on Sansome or Battery
               between Jackson and Pacific

CM 71.1   Fire House Façade Building
           1047 McAllister Street

CM 72.1   Levi Strauss Factory Building
           250 Valencia

CM74.1   Mary Ellen "Mammy" Pleasant
               Trees
           Southwest corner of Octavia
               and Bush

CM 75.1   The Chartered Bank of London
           Banking Hall
           465 California Street

APPENDIX III: DOWNTOWN-PLAN PROTECTED BUILDINGS

Article 11 of the City Planning Code offers various levels of protection for the following buildings:

SIGNIFICANT BUILDINGS—CATEGORY I:
These buildings cannot be demolished. Alterations are monitored by the Landmarks Board and the Planning Commission.

Postal Telegraph	22 Battery
Levi Strauss	98 Battery
Donohoe	99 Battery
Crown Zellerbach	1 Bush
Shell	100 Bush
Heineman	130 Bush
Standard Oil	200 Bush
Standard Oil	225 Bush
Alto	381 Bush
Pacific States	445 Bush
Fire Station #2	460 Bush
Notre Dame des	
Victoires	564 Bush
Marine	158 California
Tadich's Grill	240 California
Newhall	260 California
Robert Dollar	301 California
Harold Dollar	341 California
Bank of California	400 California
Insurance Exchange	433 California
Merchants Exchange	465 California
	554 Commercial
	564 Commercial

PG&E Substation J	569 Commercial
Continental Hotel	119 Ellis
Pickwick Hotel	67 Fifth
	231 First
Phillips	234 First
Keystone Hotel	54 First
Whiteside Apartments	150 Franklin
DeBernardi's	251 Front
	2 Geary
Schaidt	10 Geary
Rosenstock	28 Geary
Marion	108 Geary
E. Simon	120 Geary
Sacs	132 Geary
Whittell	166 Geary
St. Paul	285 Geary
Lincoln	293 Geary
Elkan Gunst	301 Geary
Geary Theater	415 Geary
Curran Theater	445 Geary
Citizen's Savings	704 Market
Bankers Investment	722 Market
Wells Fargo	744 Market
Phelan	760 Market
Humbolt	783 Market
Pacific	801 Market
Emporium	835 Market
Flood	870 Market
Hale Brothers	901 Market
	938 Market
Mechanics Savings	948 Market
Warfield Theater	982 Market

San Christina	1000 Market
Crocker Bank	1072 Market
Grant	1095 Market
Hotel Shaw	1100 Market
Orpheum Theater	1182 Market
Merchandising Mart	1301 Market
Rubyhill Vineyard	34 Mason
Kowalsky Apartments	120 Mason
	602 Mason
Hotel Mason	191 Mason
Methodist Book Concern	83 McAllister
Hastings Dormitory	100 McAllister
Argyle Hotel	132 McAllister
	447 Minna
McElnoy	54 Mint
Remedial Loan	66 Mint
Audiffred	1 Mission
	647 Mission
	658 Mission
Kean Hotel	1018 Mission
French Bank	130 Montgomery
Alexander	149 Montgomery
Mills	220 Montgomery
Russ	235 Montgomery
Bank of America	300 Montgomery
California Commercial	315 Montgomery
Kohl	400 Montgomery
Financial Center	405 Montgomery
American-Asian Bank	500 Montgomery
Paoli's	520 Montgomery
Fireman's Fund	233 Sansome
Federal Reserve	400 Sansome

Sun	401 Sansome
	407 Sansome
Rapp	121 Second
	132 Second
	141 Second
Odd Fellows	6 Seventh
	106 Sixth
Hotel Argonne	201 Sixth
Palace Garage	111 Stevenson
FAO Schwarz	46 Stockton
Macy's	101 Stockton
Schroth's	234 Stockton
Metropolitan Life	600 Stockton
French Bank	108 Sutter
Hunter-Dulin	111 Sutter
Hallidie	130 Sutter
Rose	216 Sutter
White House	255 Sutter
Sather	256 Sutter
Bemiss	266 Sutter
Hammersmith	294 Sutter
Nutall	312 Sutter
Galen	391 Sutter
Pacific Gas & Electric	445 Sutter
Pacific Gas & Electric	447 Sutter
Medical-Dental	450 Sutter
Physicians'	500 Sutter
Marines' Memorial	609 Sutter
	620 Sutter
Metropolitan	640 Sutter
Hotel California	403 Taylor
Bohemian Club	624 Taylor
	701 Taylor
Oxford Hotel	2 Turk
Masonic Temple	11 Van Ness

SIGNIFICANT BUILDINGS—CATEGORY II

These buildings are usually on very deep lots and may receive partial additions at the rear when the addition is not visible from the street.

SF Mining Exchange	350 Bush
	430 Bush
SF Environmental Center	530 Bush
Twenty California	20 California
Hind	230 California
Welch	244 California
YMCA	166 Embarcadero
Sussex	450 Geary
	458 Geary
KGO	255 Golden Gate
William Volker	631 Howard
Dettner's Printing	835 Howard
Eng Skell	1035 Howard
	1126 Howard
Young	123 Kearny
Palace Hotel	633 Market

CONTRIBUTING BUILDINGS—CATEGORY III

Retention of these buildings is urged, but not mandated.

Notre Dame des Victoires	566 Bush
Old U.S. Mint	608 Commercial
	33 Drumm
	42 Fell
	342 Howard
	667 Howard
Blindcraft	1097 Howard
Guilfoy Cornice	1234 Howard
Central Tower	703 Market
	1083 Market
	1582 Market
Jack's Restaurant	615 Sacramento
Seneca Hotel	32 Sixth
California Farmer	83 Stevenson
Brizzard & Young	72 Tehema
J.S. Godau	1 United Nations Plaza
	41 Van Ness

CONTRIBUTING BUILDINGS—CATEGORY IV

Retention of these buildings is urged.

	28 Belden
	40 Belden
	52 Belden
Sam's Grill	364 Bush
Shasta Hotel	380 Bush
	415 Bush
	429 Bush
Hansa Hotel	447 Bush
Mfg. Jewelers	461 Bush
St. Charles Hotel	507 Bush
Terbush	515 Bush
	553 Clay
	559 Clay
John's Grill	61 Ellis
Powell	111 Ellis
Misses Butler	120 Ellis
	222 Front
	235 Front
Schroeder's	236 Front
	239 Front
	246 Front
	250 Front
Hotel Graystone	66 Geary
Cailleau	88 Geary
Granat Brothers	100 Geary
Paragon	101 Geary
	129 Geary
	146 Geary
	152 Geary
	156 Geary
Werner	251 Geary
Hotel Stewart	347 Geary
Rosebud's English Pub	366 Geary
	381 Geary
Paisley Hotel	418 Geary
Somerton Hotel	436 Geary
	459 Geary
	468 Geary
Hotel David	476 Geary
	484 Geary
Hotel Maryland	490 Geary
	485 Pine
Guggenheim	216 Post
Gump's	228 Post
Graff	233 Post
Mercedes	251 Post
	272 Post
	438 Post
Hotel Cecil	545 Post
J. J. Moore Apts.	620 Post
	624 Post
	45 Powell
Hotel Golden State	100 Powell
	111 Powell
	120 Powell
Elevated Shops	134 Powell
Hotel Herbert	151 Powell
Villa Florence Hotel	201 Powell
Howard	207 Powell
	226 Powell
	235 Powell
	236 Powell
Hotel Stratford	421 Powell
United Airlines	435 Powell
	439 Powell
	445 Powell
	558 Sacramento
	560 Sacramento
PG&E Station J	568 Sacramento
Potter	576 Sacramento
Fugazi Bank	415 Sansome
Schwabacher	20 Second
Morgan	36 Second
	42 Second
Kentfield & Esser	48 Second
	52 Second
	60 Second
	70 Second
	76 Second
	90 Second
	120 Second
Morton L. Cook	133 Second
	144 Second
	149 Second

APPENDIX IV: CALIFORNIA REGISTERED HISTORICAL LANDMARKS IN SAN FRANCISCO

79 Presidio of San Francisco
Moraga Avenue, The Presidio

80 Montgomery Block (Demolished)
Lobby, 600 Montgomery Street

81 Landing Place of Captain J. B.
Montgomery
Montgomery and Clay streets

82 Castillo De San Joaquin
Fort Point

83 Shoreline Markers
Battery, Bush, and Market streets

84 Rincon Hill
First Street between Harrison and
Bryant streets

85 Office of the *Star* Newspaper
Washington and Walter Lum Place

86 California Theater
North side of Bush Street between
Kearny Street and Grant Avenue

87 Site of First U. S. Branch Mint in
California
608 Commercial Street
(San Francisco Landmark No. 34)

88 Niantic Hotel (Building)
Clay and Sansome streets

89 Site of Parrott Granite Block
NW corner of California and
Montgomery streets

90 Fort Gunnybags
Sacramento between Davis and Front
streets

91 Telegraph Hill

119 Portsmouth Plaza
In park on Kearny, between Clay and
Washington streets

192 El Dorado, Parker House, and
Dennison's Exchange
Merchant and Kearny streets

236 Entrance of the *San Carlos* into San
Francisco Bay
Aquatic Park, foot of Van Ness
Avenue

327 Mission San Francisco De Asis
(Mission Dolores)
Dolores between 16th Street and
Chula Lane
(San Francisco Landmark No. 1)

328 Long Wharf
Commercial Street west of
Montgomery Street

408 Site of the First Meeting of
Freemasons Held in California
726 Montgomery Street

453 Lucas, Turner & Company (Sherman's
Bank)
Montgomery and Jackson streets
(San Francisco Landmark No. 26)

454 Woodward's Gardens
Mission and Duboce streets

459 Site of brick building of the firm of
Mellus and Howard
Montgomery and Clay streets

462 Site of First Jewish Religious Services
in San Francisco
Montgomery between Washington and
Jackson streets

500 Eastern Terminus of Clay Street Hill
Railroad
Portsmouth Plaza, Clay and Kearny
streets

587 First Public School
Portsmouth Plaza, Clay and
Walter Lum Place

623 Union Square
Geary and Powell streets

650 Site of What Cheer House
Sacramento at Leidesdorff Street

691 Sarcophagus of Thomas Starr King
Franklin Street between Starr King
Way and Geary Street

696 Western Business Headquarters of
Russell, Majors and Waddell,
Founders, Owners and Operators of
the Pony Express
617 Montgomery Street

754 Site of the Mark Hopkins Institute of
Art
California at Mason Street

772 Original Site of St. Mary's College
College Avenue at Mission Street and
Crescent Avenue

784 El Camino Real
(As Father Serra Knew It and Helped
Blaze It)

Mission San Diego de Alcala, San
Diego, to Mission San Francisco de
Asis

810 Old St. Mary's Church
California Street at Grant Avenue
(San Francisco Landmark No. 2)

819 Hudson's Bay Company Headquarters
Montgomery between Sacramento and
Commercial streets

841 The Conservatory
Golden Gate Park
(San Francisco Landmark No. 50)

861 Site of the first California State Fair
Bush at Montgomery Street

875 Old United States Mint
5th at Mission Street

876 City of Paris Building (Demolished)
Geary at Stockton Street

937 Site of the Invention of the
Three Reel Bell Slot Machine
Battery at Market Street

941 Farnsworth's Laboratory (Co-inventor
of Television)
Green at Sansome Street

964 Birthplace of the United Nations
(War Memorial buildings)
Van Ness Avenue between McAllister
and Hayes streets
(San Francisco Landmark No. 84)

974 Golden Gate Bridge

STATE OF CALIFORNIA POINTS OF
HISTORICAL INTEREST IN
SAN FRANCISCO

Holy Cross Parish Hall
1820 Eddy Street
(San Francisco Landmark No. 6)

St Patrick's Church
Mission, between Third and Fourth streets
(San Francisco Landmark No. 4)

St. Francis of Assisi Church
Vallejo Street at Columbus Avenue
(San Francisco Landmark No. 5)

Bank of California
    California at Sansome Street
    (San Francisco Landmark No. 3)

South San Francisco Opera House
    Mendell Street and Newcomb Avenue
    (San Francisco Landmark No. 8)

Audiffred Building
    Mission Street at The Embarcadero
    (San Francisco Landmark No. 7)

Haas-Lilienthal House
    2007 Franklin Street
    (San Francisco Landmark No. 69)

U.S. Public Health Service Hospital
    15th Avenue at Lake Street

Francis Scott Key Statue
    Music Concourse, Golden Gate Park
    (San Francisco Landmark No. 96)

Visitacion Valley Community Center
    66 Raymond Avenue

Site of the Birthplace of Alice B. Toklas
    922 O'Farrell Street

Washington Hall
    At the Plaza (now known as Portsmouth
    Square)

APPENDIX V: SITES ON THE NATIONAL REGISTER OF HISTORIC PLACES IN SAN FRANCISCO

Alma (Scow Schooner)
    2905 Hyde Street
Alcatraz
    (Alcatraz Island National Historic Park)
    San Francisco Bay
Aquatic Park Historic District
    Bounded by Van Ness Avenue, Hyde and
    Polk streets
Atherton House
    1990 California Street
    (San Francisco Landmark No. 70)
Audiffred Building
    1 Mission Street
    (San Francisco Landmark No. 7)
Balclutha
    (*Star of Alaska, Pacific Queen,* sailing ship
    Balclutha)
    Pier 41 East
Bank of Italy
    552 Montgomery Street
Beach Chalet
    1000 The Great Highway
    (San Francisco Landmark No. 179)
C. A. Belden House
    2004 Gough Street
Belt Railroad Engine House and Sandhouse
    (Belt Railroad Roundhouse and Sandhouse)
    Lombard and Sansome streets and
    The Embarcadero
    (San Francisco Landmark No. 114)
Building at 1735–1737 Webster Street
Building at 1840–1842 Eddy Street
Building at 33–35 Beideman Place
Building at 45–57 Beideman Place
Bush Street–Cottage Row Historic District
    2101–2125 Bush Street, 1–6 Cottage Row
    and 1940–1948 Sutter Street

C. A. Thayer (Lumber Schooner)
    San Francisco Maritime State
    Historical Park
Callam-Merritt House
    2355 Washington Street
Calvary Presbyterian Church
    2501 Fillmore Street
    (San Francisco Landmark No. 103)
Chambord Apartments
    1298 Sacramento Street
    (San Francisco Landmark No. 106)
City of Paris building (Demolished)
    181–199 Geary Street
Delane House
    70 Buena Vista Terrace
Frank G. Edwards House
    1366 Guerrero Street
    (San Francisco Landmark No. 189)
Engine House Number 31
Eureka (*Ukiah,* ferryboat *Eureka*)
    San Francisco Maritime State Historic Park
    2905 Hyde Street
Farallone Islands
    28 miles west of San Francisco
Federal Reserve Bank of San Francisco (Old)
    400 Sansome Street
    (San Francisco Landmark No. 158)
Ferry Station Post Office Building
    Agriculture Building
    The Embarcadero at Mission Street
Feusier Octagon House (Kenny Octagon
    House)
    1067 Green Street
    (San Francisco Landmark No. 36)
Fillmore-Pine Building
    Southeast corner of Fillmore at Pine Street
Delia Fleishacker Memorial Building

Zoo Road at Sloat Boulevard
James C. Flood Mansion
    California at Mason Street
    (San Francisco Landmark No. 64)
Fort Mason Historic District
    Bounded by Van Ness Avenue, Bay and
    Laguna streets
Fort Miley Military Reservation
    (Point Lobos Military Reservation)
Fort Point National Historic Site
    North tip of San Francisco Peninsula
Geary Theater (Columbia Theater)
    415 Geary Street
    (San Francisco Landmark No. 82)
Girls Club
    362 Capp Street
Golden Gate Park Conservatory
    John F. Kennedy Drive
    (San Francisco Landmark No. 50)
Goodman Building (Joseph Emeric Building)
    1117 Geary Street
    (San Francisco Landmark No. 71)
Griffing's Frederick (ship)
    Gold Rush ship beneath Levi's Plaza
Haas-Lilienthal House
    2007 Franklin Street
    (San Francisco Landmark No. 69)
Hale Brothers Department Store
    901 Market Street
Hallidie Building
    130 Sutter Street
    (San Francisco Landmark No. 37)
Haslett Warehouse
    680 Beach Street
    (San Francisco Landmark No. 59)
Herald Hotel
    303 Eddy Street

Hercules (tugboat)
  Hyde Street Pier
House at 1239–1245 Scott Street
House at 1249–1251 Scott Street
House at 1254–56 Montgomery Street
House at 1321 Scott Street
House at 1331–1335 Scott Street
House at 584 Page Street
International Hotel (Demolished)
  848 Kearny Street
Jackson Square Historic District
  Bounded by Broadway, Sansome and
  Washington streets and Columbus Avenue
Jessie Street Substation
  220 Jessie Street
  (San Francisco Landmark No. 87)
Koshland House
  3800 Washington Street
  (San Francisco Landmark No. 95)
Krotoszyner House and Office
  995 Sutter Street
Lewis Ark (houseboat)
  Hyde Street Pier
Liberty Street Historic District
  15–188 Liberty Street
Lotta's Fountain
  Geary, Market, and Kearny streets
  (San Francisco Landmark No. 73)
Lydia (old whaling bark *Lydia*)
  King Street at The Embarcadero
Market Street Theater and Loft District
  982–1112 Market Street,
  973–1105 Market Street
  1 Jones Street, 1–35 Taylor Street
McElroy Octagon House
  2645 Gough Street
  (San Francisco Landmark No. 17)
John McMullen House
  827 Guerrero Street
  (San Francisco Landmark No. 123)
Mills Building and Tower
  220 Montgomery and 220 Bush streets
  (San Francisco Landmark No. 76)
Mish House
  1153 Oak Street
  (San Francisco Landmark No. 62)
Mission Dolores (Mission San Francisco
  De Asis)
  320 Dolores Street
  (San Francisco Landmark No. 1)
Moss Flats Building
  1626 The Great Highway
Myrtle Street Flats
  234–248 Myrtle Street
National Carbon Company Building
  599 Eighth Street

Old Ohio Street Houses
  17–55 Osgood Place
Old U.S. Mint
  Fifth at Mission Street
PG&E Substation J
  569 Commercial Street
  (San Francisco Landmark No. 142)
Paige Motor Car Company
  1699 Van Ness Avenue
Park View Hotel
  750 Stanyan Street
Theodore F. Payne House
  1409 Sutter Street
Abner Phelps House
  1111 Oak Street
  (San Francisco Landmark No. 32)
Pioneer Trunk Factory
  2195–2199 Folsom Street/3180 18th Street
Pioneer Woolen Mill and D. Ghirardelli
  Company
  900 North Point Street
  (San Francisco Landmark No. 30)
Point Lobos Archeological Sites
  Address restricted
Presidio of San Francisco
  Northern tip of San Francisco Peninsula
Pumping Station Number 2
  North end of Van Ness Avenue
Rincon Annex
  101–199 Mission Street
  (San Francisco Landmark No. 107)
Russian Hill-Macondry Lane District
Russian Hill-Paris Block Architectural District
Russian Hill Vallejo-Street Crest District
SS Jeremiah O'Brien
  Pier 3, Ft. Mason Center
SS Rio de Janeiro
  Address restricted
St. Joseph's Church and Complex
  1401–1415 Howard Street
  (San Francisco Landmark No. 120)
St. Joseph's Hospital
  355 Buena Vista Avenue East
St. Paulus Lutheran Church
  999 Eddy Street
  (San Francisco Landmark No. 116)
San Francisco Cable Cars
  1390 Washington Street
San Francisco Civic Center Historic District
  Bounded by Golden Gate Avenue,
  Franklin, Hayes, and Market streets
San Francisco National Guard Armory and
  Arsenal (State Armory and Arsenal)
  1800 Mission Street
  (San Francisco Landmark No. 108)
San Francisco Port of Embarcation

(See also Ft. Mason)
  Ft. Mason
Schoenstein Organ Building
  3101 20th Street
  (San Francisco Landmark No. 99)
Irving Murray Scott School
  (Potrero School)
  1060 Tennessee Street
  (San Francisco Landmark No. 138)
Ship *King Phillip*–schooner *Reporter*
(shipwreck site)
  Foot of Ortega Street
Six-Inch Rifle Gun No. 9
  Baker Beach
Southern Pacific Company Hospital Historic
  District
  1400 Fell Street
Stadmuller House
  819 Eddy Street
  (San Francisco Landmark No. 35)
Sutter Street 1813–1813B
The Real Estate Associates (TREA) Houses
  2503, 2524, 2530, and 2536 Clay Street
Trinity Presbyterian Church
  3261 23rd Street
  (San Francisco Landmark No. 166)
Tubbs Cordage Company Office Building
  Hyde Street Pier
Union Ferry Depot (The Ferry Building)
  Foot of Market Street at The Embarcadero
  (San Francisco Landmark No. 90)
U.S. Customhouse
  555 Battery Street
U.S. Post Office and Courthouse
  Seventh at Mission Street
USS *Pampanito* (SS 383)
  Pier 45
Wampa
  Hyde Street Pier
Russell Warren House
  465–467 Oak Street
William Westerfeld House
  1198 Fulton Street
  (San Francisco Landmark No. 135)
Whittier Mansion
  2090 Jackson Street
  (San Francisco Landmark No. 75)
Albert Wilford Houses
  2121 Vallejo Street
YMCA Hotel
  351 Turk Street

INDEX

Note: *Italic* page numbers refer to illustrations. Landmarks are indexed by name and by street.

Alamo Square Historic District, 14, 198, 219, 287; *287*
Albion Ale and Porter Brewery, 102; *102*
Alemany, Abp. Joseph, 21, 177
Alhambra (Spain), 283
American Conservatory Theater, 128
American Protestant Association, 27
Annie Street, 23
Anthony, Earl C., Packard Showroom, 221; *221*
apartment house, 158
apothecary, 257
Applegarth, George: Spreckles Mansion, 285; *284–85*
Archbishop's Mansion, 219; *218*
Architect and Engineer (journal), 192
Arguella Street, 250
Arguello, Don Luis Antonio, 17
armory, 163
Art Deco/Art Moderne Style, 10, 163
Arts and Crafts Movement, 10, 178
Association for the Improvement and Adornment of San Francisco, 291
Atherton, Mr. and Mrs. Faxton Dean, 115
Atherton, Faxton Dean, 289
Atherton House, 115; *114*
Atkinson, Joseph M., 148
Atkinson House, 148; *149*
Audiffred Building, 23; *22*
Audiffret, Hippolite d', 23
Augusta, Mother, 197
automobile showrooms, 220, 221
Axford House, 194; *195*
Ayala, Capt. Juan Manuel de, 289

Babson, Seth: Stone House, 123; *122*
Baker and Hamilton Building (Sutton and Weeks), 278; *278*
Baker Street, 138
Bakewell and Brown: California School of Fine Arts, 133; *133;* San Francisco City Hall, 42; *43*
Banco Populare Italiano Operaia Fugazi (Paff), 89; *88*
Bank of America, 89
Bank of California (Bliss and Faville), 19; *19*
Bank of Canton, 63
Bank of Italy, 83, 89, 220
Bank of Lucas, Turner & Company (Clark), 49; *48*

banks, 19, 49, 89, 164, 190, 192, 193, 228
Barbary Coast, 289
Barnard, Thomas, 57
Barth, Herman, 186: Brandenstein House, 186; *186–87*
Battery Street, 157, 161, 289
Bauer, John, 190
Bauer & Schweitzer Malting Company, 190; *190*
Bay Street, 98, 138
Bayview District, 102, 105
Beach Chalet (Polk), 267; *267*
Beach Street, 101
Beaux-Arts Style, 130, 158, 164, 170, 175
Belli, Melvin, 27
Belli Annex, 27; *27*
Belli Building, 27; *26*
Belt Line Railroad Roundhouse, 169; *168–69*
Berry Street, 279
Bethlehem Steel Shipyards, 15
Biedeman Place Historic District, 13
blacksmith shop, 214
Blackstone Court Historic District, 291; *290*
Blackstone House, 291
Bliss and Faville: Bank of California, 19; *19;* Columbia Theater, 128; *129;* Savings Union Bank, 192; *192*
Blyth-Zellerbach Committee, 260
B'nai David Synagogue, 175
Borel, Antoine, 164
Borel Building (Pissis), 164; *164*
Bourne, William B., 69
Bourne Mansion (Polk), 69; *68*
Boy's High School, 200
Brandenstein, Max, 186
Brandenstein (Bransten) House (Barth), 186; *186–87*
Brandon, E. J., 161
Bransten, Edward (*né* Brandenstein), 186
Bransten, Florine (*née* Haas), 186
Brenham, Charles, 289
breweries, 102, 190
bridge, 279
British Motors, 221; *221*
Broadway, 148
Brown, A. Page: Ferry Building, 141; *140;* Queen House, 285; Trinity Episcopal Church, 109; *108*
Brown, Arthur, Jr.: California School of Fine Arts, 133; *133;* San Francisco City Hall, 42; *43;* War Memorial Opera House and Veterans Building (with G. Albert Lansburgh), 130, 175; *130–31*
brownstone, 106
Buchanan Street, 81, 98, 111, 215
Buena Vista Vinacultural Society, 31
Buich Building (Crim and Scott), 208; *209*
Bulkhead Saloon, 23
Bull, Alpheus, Jr.: Dutch Windmill, 213; *212*
Burnell, John Hamlin, 102

Burnham, Daniel, 291
Burnham and Root: Mills Building, 12, 118; *119*
Burr, Anna (*née* Barnard), 57
Burr, Edmond, 57
Burr, Ephraim William, 57, 289
Burr House (Wharff), 57; *56*
Bush Street, 75, 109, 111, 118, 128, 170, 207, 248, 260
Bush Street Temple (Lyon), 128; *128*

Cable Car Barn and Powerhouse, 76; *76*
Cable Car Clothiers. *See* Savings Union Bank
cable car systems, 76
Cadillac Hotel (Meyer and O'Brien), 262; *262*
Cahill, B. J. S., 291
Cahill Plan, 291
Calhoun Terrace, 10
California Culinary Academy, 258
California Hall, 258; *259*
California Historical Society (Swain), 123; *123*
California Hotel and Theater, 75
California Registered Historical Landmarks, 18, 86, 295–96
California School of Fine Arts (Bakewell and Brown), 133; *133*
California Shingle Style, 10, 79, 243, 283
California Street, 18, 19, 91, 93, 95, 106, 115, 208, 244
Callister, Charles Warren: addition, First Unitarian Church, 71
Calvary Presbyterian Church (McDougall and McDougall), 160; *160*
Cameron, Donaldina, House, 77; *77*
Campfire Girls Building (Gutterson), 250; *250*
car house, 256
Carpenter Gothic Style, 9, 81
carriage houses, 182, 194, 239, 280
Carson House (Eureka), 198
Casebolt, Henry, 85
Casebolt House, 85; *84*
Castro Street, 154
Castro Theater (Miller and Pflueger), 154; *155*
cathedrals, 18, 23, 53, 246
Chambers, Richard Craig, 176
Chambers Mansion (Mathews; Sawyer), 176; *176*
Chambord Apartments (Dunn), 158; *159*
Château de Blois (France), 54
Chestnut Street, 133
Chevra Mikvah Israel and B'nai David Synagogue, 175
Chicago School, 118
Chicago World's Fair (1893), 190, 224
Chinatown Historic District [Proposed], 14, 288; *288*
Chinatown YWCA (Morgan), 180; *180*
Chocolate Factory, 54

Chris' Cafeteria Building (Crim and Scott), 208; *209*
churches, 12, 17, 18, 23, 53, 70, 71, 72, 109, 132, 160, 172, 177, 243, 246, 248, 255, 263
Church Street, 70
Circle Gallery. *See* Morris Store
City Beautiful Movement, 136, 207, 224
City Hall. *See* San Francisco City Hall
City of Paris department store, 12, 193
City Planning Code, 11
civic buildings, 42, 130, 138. *See also under* Golden Gate Park
Civic Center (Kelham), 37
Civic Center Historic District [Proposed], 14, 130, 291; *290*
Clark, Reuben: Bank of Lucas, Turner & Company, 49; *48*
Clarke, Alfred E., 126
Clarke Mansion (Clarke's Folly), 126; *127*
Classical Revival Style, 42, 126, 136, 170, 186, 190, 193, 201, 207, 221, 228, 243, 263
Clay Street, 76, 180
Clay Street Center and Residence Club (Morgan), 180; *180*
Clayton, Joel, 78
clock, 121
Clocktower, 54
clubhouses, 264, 267
Clunie, Thomas J., 189
Clunie House (Curlett), 189; *188*
Coast Savings (Howard), 164; *165*
Coit, Lillie Hitchcock, 240
Coit Tower, 10, 240; *241*
Coleman, Edward, 93
Coleman House (Salfield and Kohlberg), 93; *92*
Coleman, John C., 91, 93
Colonial Dames Octagon House-Museum, 34; *35*
Columbia Theater (Bliss and Faville), 128; *129*
Columbus Avenue, 61, 89
Commerce Street, 289
commercial buildings, 23, 27, 28, 29, 30, 31, 33, 38, 41, 45, 49, 54, 58, 61, 66, 102, 115, 116, 118, 154, 161, 164, 170, 175, 189, 190, 214, 216, 222, 224, 227, 230, 233, 234, 236, 243, 257, 260, 278, 289. *See also* automobile showrooms; banks; hotels; restaurants; theaters; transportation buildings; utility buildings; warehouses
Commercial Street, 63, 204
community center and service agency buildings, 53, 77, 135, 167, 180, 250, 258, 267
Comstock Mines, 19, 106, 184, 216, 273
conservatories, 86, 124
Conservatory, The, 86; *86–87*
consulate buildings, 45, 47
Cooper, Dr. Elias S., 170
Coppola, Francis Ford, 61
cottages, 111
Crabtree, Lotta, 27, 83, 120

Craftsman Style, 10, 211
Cram, Ralph Adam, 246
Cravath, Ruth, Studio, Home, and Stoneyard, 211
Crim and Scott: Chris' Cafeteria Building, 208: *209*
Crocker Building, 222
Crockett, Joseph B.: San Francisco Gas Light Company, 98; *99*
Crown Zellerbach Complex and Site (Skidmore, Owings & Merrill), 10, 260; *261*
Crown Zellerbach Plaza, 222
Curlett, William: Clunie House, 189; *188*

Dailey, Gardiner: addition, Haas-Lilienthal House, 112
Day, Clinton, 193: Union Trust Bank, 193; *193*
De Haro Street, 135
DeMartini, John, 83
designated structures of merit, 293
Deutsches Haus, Das, 258; *259*
Dickenson, John, 137
Dietle, Charles, 83
Dietle House (Geilfuss), 83
Divisadero Street, 58, 105, 257, 280
Dodge and Dolliver: St. John's Presbyterian Church, 132; *132*
Dolores Street, 17, 111, 202
Don Lee Building, 220; *220*
Donohoe, Joseph, 31
Dougherty, James Witt, 158
Douglass Street, 126
Dovre Hall, 267
Downtown Plan, 14; protected buildings, 293–94
Doyle, R., & Sons, 136
Dunn, James Francis: Chambord Apartments, 158; *159*
Durham Cathedral (England), 109
Dutch Windmill (Bull), 213; *212*
Dutton, Henry, Jr., 97
Dutton, Mary (*née* Talbot), 97

earthquake and fire of 1906, 10; buildings that survived intact, 23, 25, 28, 61, 65, 72, 79, 106, 109, 158; Engine Company No. 22 role, 53; Fire Chief Sullivan's death, 75; first brick building after, 50; refugee shacks, 251; shelters, 70, 72
East Coast influences, 9, 10, 111
Eastlake Style, 10, 81, 115
Eco della Patria (newspaper), 31
Ecole des Beaux-Arts (Paris), 42, 170, 180, 243
Eddy Street, 20, 23, 63, 169, 172, 262
Edwardian Style, 10, 160, 211, 264
Edwards, Frank G., 276
Edwards House, 276; *277*

18th Street, 197, 267
Embarcadero, 141, 169
Emeric, Joseph, 115
Emeric Building, 115; *115*
Emerson, Ralph Waldo, 71
Empire Malt House, 190; *190*
Empire Mining Company, 69
Equitable Building, 260
Exposition Auditorium, 200, 291

factory, 189
Fair, James, 273
Fairmont Hotel (Reid Brothers), 273; *272–73*
Fair Oaks Street, 278, 292
Family Service Agency (Maybeck), 167; *166–67*
Federal Reserve Bank, early type, 63
Federal Reserve Bank Building (Kelham), 228; *228*
Feinstein, Dianne, 14
Fell Street, 200, 275
Felton, Kitty, 167
Ferry Building (Brown; Schweinforth), 141, 285; *140*
Feusier Octagon House, 65; *64*
Fifth Street, 63
Fillmore Street, 158, 160
Filoli (Polk), 69
Financial District, 12, 13, 204
Finnish Gethsemane Lutheran Church, 70
fire chief's residence, 75; *74*
firehouses: Engine Company No. 8 (Reid), 271; *271;* Engine Company No. 21 (Henriksen and Mahoney), 136, 137; *136;* Engine Company No. 22, 53; *53;* Engine Company No. 23 (Henriksen and Mahoney), 137; *137;* Engine Company No. 37 (Ward), 270; *270;* Station 2, 207; *206*
fire of 1851, 41
First Congregational Church (Reid Brothers), 263; *263*
First Street, 151
First Unitarian Church (Perry), 71; *71;* King sculpture, 211
Fitzhugh Building, 12
Flatiron Building (Havens), 182, 222; *223*
Flood, James Clair, 106, 170
Flood, James, Jr., 216
Flood Building (Pissis), 216; *217*
Flood Mansion (Laver; Polk), 106; *107*
Flugger, Charles: Hanson House, 283
Folger's Coffee, 227
Folsom Street, 137, 214
forty-niners, 9, 81
Foster, Arthur, 132
Foundation for San Francisco's Architectural Heritage, 85, 112
fountain, 120
Fourteenth Street, 163

Fowler, Orson Squire, 34
Fox Theater, 12
Franciscan Fathers, 9, 255
Francisco Street, 190
Franklin Street, 71, 93, 112, 186
Fremery, James, 289
"French Church." See Notre Dame des
    Victoires
French Renaissance Revival Style, 42
Front Street, 143, 289
Fugazi, John F., 89
Fuller, George A., Construction Company, 163
Fuller-O'Brien Paint Company, 123
Fulton Street, 53, 198, 219

Gallagher, Rev. Hugh, 177
Ganella, Joseph, 27
Ganella Building, 27; 27
Garden Court. See Palace Hotel
Gaylord Hotel, 229; 229
Gazotte, Charles De, 45
Geary Street, 71, 115, 120, 128, 283
Geary Theater (Bliss and Faville), 128; 129
Geilfuss, Henry: Dietle House, 83; St. Mark's
    Evangelical Lutheran Church, 72; 73;
    Westerfeld House, 198; 199
General Engineering and Drydock Company, 289
Geneva Car Barn, 256; 256
Genthe, Arnold, 34
Georgian Style, 186
German Renaissance Style, 53, 258
Ghirardelli, Domingo, 289
Ghirardelli Building, 31; 31
Ghirardelli Building Annex, 33; 32
Ghirardelli, D., Company, 31, 33, 54; 54–55
Ghirardelli Square (Wurster, Bernardi, and
    Evans), 54, 101; 54–55
Gibb, Daniel, 143, 289
Gibb-Sanborn Warehouses, 143; 142
Golden Era (newspaper), 41
Golden Era Building, 41; 40
Golden Gate Avenue, 255
Golden Gate Bridge, 279
Golden Gate Park: Beach Chalet, 267; 267;
    Conservatory, 86; 86–87; Dutch Windmill,
    213; 212; Francis Scott Key Monument,
    146; 146; Lawn Bowling Clubhouse and
    Greens, 264; 265; Park Superintendent's
    Residence, 253; 252–53; Sharon Building,
    184; 184–85
Golden Gate Park Concourse, 146
Golden Gateway Center, 13, 260
Gold Rush era, 9, 143, 288, 289
Goodman, Abraham and Sarah, 115
Goodman Building, 155; 155
Gothic Revival Style, 18, 20, 95, 172,
    222, 246
Gottlob and Marx, 128
Gough Street, 34, 167

government buildings, 42, 63, 163
Grace Cathedral Close (Hobart), 246;
    246–47
Grand Central Terminal (New York), 11
Grant Avenue, 192, 201, 288
Great Highway, The, 213, 267
Green, Theodore, Apothecary (Newsom),
    257; 257
greenhouse, 86
Green Street, 65, 83, 189, 289
Greenwich Street, 157, 178
Griffing, Frederick, wharf, 289
Grogan, Alexander B., 50, 289
Grogan-Lent-Atherton Building, 50; 51
Grove Street, 130, 200
Guerrero, Francisco, 111
Guerrero Street, 181, 194, 215, 276
Guggenheim Building, 186
Guggenheim Museum (Wright), 116
Gutterson, Henry: Campfire Girls Building,
    250; 250

Haas, William, 112, 186
Haas Brothers, Inc., 186
Haas-Lilienthal House (Schmidt), 112; 113
Haight Street, 239
Hale, Edward Everett, 71
Hallidie, Andrew S., 66, 71, 76
Hallidie Building (Polk), 66, 116, 222; 67
Hall of Justice, 12
Halprin, Lawrence, 54
Hammersmith Building (Lansburgh), 175;
    174
Hanson House (Flugger), 283
Harrison Street, 227
Harte, Bret, 27, 41, 71
Haslett Warehouse (Mooser), 101; 100
Havens, Charles, 292: Flatiron Building, 222;
    223; Havens Mansion and Carriage House,
    182; 183
Havens and Topke, 182
Havens Mansion and Carriage House
    (Havens), 182; 183
Hayes Street, 275
Hayward, Alvinza, 233
Health Sciences Library. See Lane Library
Hearst, George, 170
Hearst, William Randolph, 180
Heidelberg Castle (Germany), 258
Hemenway and Miller: Italian Swiss Colony
    Warehouse, 157; 156–57
Henriksen and Mahoney: firehouses: Engine
    Company No. 21, 136; 136; Engine
    Company No. 23, 137; 137
Herbert, Beatrice, 83
Here Today (survey report), 11, 85
Heritage (foundation), 13
Hermann, John, 258
Hermann Safe Company, 258

Herzka and Knowles, 260
Hibernia Bank (Pissis), 190; 191
High School of Commerce (Reid), 200; 200
Hill Street, 292. See also Liberty/Hill Historic
    District
Hills, Austin and Reuben, 227
Hills Brothers Coffee Building (Kelham),
    227; 226
Hinckle, Charles L., 280
Hinckle House and Carriage House, 280; 281
Historic Districts, 10, 12, 14, 287–92
Hobart, Lewis: Grace Cathedral Close, 246;
    246–47; Mills Building, 118; 119
Hobart Building (Polk), 222, 236; 237
Hoffman Grill Building, 205; 205
Holy Cross Parish Hall. See Old St. Patrick's
    Church
Home for All, A (book; Fowler), 34
Home Telephone Company, 201; 201
Hopkins, Mark, 170, 268
hospital complex, 275
Hotaling, Anson, 289
Hotaling, A. P., and Sons, 28, 29, 38
Hotaling Annex East, 29; 29
Hotaling Annex West, 38; 39
Hotaling Building, 28, 29; 28
Hotaling Place, 28, 38
Hotaling Stables Building, 28
hotels, 37, 47, 83, 262, 268, 273
house-museums, 34, 112
House of the Flag, 79; 79
houses, 34, 57, 58, 63, 65, 78, 79, 81, 83,
    85, 91, 93, 95, 97, 102, 105, 111, 112,
    115, 123, 126, 147, 148, 153, 169, 181,
    186, 189, 194, 198, 211, 239, 244, 251,
    276, 278, 280, 283, 285. See also mansions
Howard, John Galen: Italian American Bank
    Building, 164; 165
Howard Street, 177
Howe, Julia Ward, 71
Hunter's Point Springs and Albion Brewery,
    102; 102
Huntington Social Hall, 275
Hyde Street, 53, 101

Independent Wood Company, 161; 161
Innes Avenue, 102
International Russian Orthodox Church, 53
International Style, 10, 169
Iron Cornicemakers Union, 214
Islam Temple (Ross), 283; 282–83
Italian American Bank Building (Howard),
    164; 165
Italianate Style, 10, 38, 57, 78, 83, 85, 91,
    95, 97, 102, 105, 126, 153, 169, 197, 198,
    276, 287
Italian Swiss Colony Warehouse (Hemenway
    and Miller), 157; 156–57

Jackson Square, 10, 41, 45, 47
Jackson Square Historic District, 12, 14, 289; *288*
Jackson Street, 12, 28, 29, 30, 31, 33, 38, 45, 47, 49, 50, 95, 123, 289
Jack's Restaurant, 211; *210*
Jefferson Street, 138
Jesse Alley, 234
Jessie Street Substation (Polk), 13, 136; *8*
John F. Kennedy Drive, 86, 213, 253
Johnson, Walter S., 138
Jones Alley, 28
Jones Street, 190, 229
Joost, Anna (*née* Miller), 126
Joost, Behrend, 126
Julius' Castle (Mastropasqua), 178; *179*

Kahlman, Harold, 13
KBS (Jewish order), 27
Kearny Street, 61, 75, 120, 208
Kelham, George: Federal Reserve Bank Building, 228; *228;* Hills Brothers Coffee Building, 227; *226;* Palace Hotel, 37; *36–37*
Kenny, George L., 65
Kenny Octagon House, 65; *64*
Kerrigan, Frank W., 211
Kerrigan House, 211
Kershaw House, 194; *195*
Key, Francis Scott, Monument (Story), 146; *146*
Keyser and Brown (builders): Bank of Lucas, Turner & Company, 49; *48*
King, Thomas Starr, 71, 211
Klokars, Edwin, 214
Klokars Blacksmith Shop, 214; *214*
Knickerbocker Trust Company Bank (New York), 19
Knoll International, 41
Kohl Building (Percy and Polk), 233; *232*
Koshland, Mr. and Mrs. Marcus, 147
Koshland House (Van Trees), 10, 147, 285; *147*
Kraft, Julius A.: St. Paulus Lutheran Church, 172; *173*
Kroeber, Alfred, 169
Kuh, Frederick, 189

Labault, Lucien, 267
Lafayette Guard, 41
Lagauterie, C., and Company, 45, 49
Lagen, Alice, 239
Lagen, Dr. John, 239
Lagen, Katie (*née* McMorry), 239
Laguna Street, 23, 98, 239
Lake Street, 132
Lane Library (Pissis), 170; *171*
Langerman's Building, 27; *26*
Lansburgh, G. Albert: Hammersmith Building, 175; *174;* War Memorial Opera House and Veterans Building (with Arthur Brown, Jr.), 130, 175; *130–31*
Larco, Nicholas, 45
Larco's Building, 45; *44*
Larkin Street, 54, 200
Laver, Augustus: Flood Mansion, 106; *107*
Lawn Bowling Clubhouse and Greens, 264; *265*
Leale, Capt. John, 78
Leale House, 78; *78*
Leavenworth Street, 262
Lee, Don, Building, 220; *220*
Lent, William M., 50, 289
Levi Plaza, 289
Levi Strauss & Co., 157, 161
Lewis, David, 270
Lewis House, 270; *270*
Lexington Street, 292
"Liberty" (sculpture; Pattigan), 192
Liberty/Hill Historic District, 14, 194, 292; *292*
Liberty Street, 292
library, 170
Lick, James, 86, 146; Estate, 81
Lilienthal, Alice (*née* Haas), 112
Lilienthal, Ernest L., 95
Lilienthal, Estelle (*née* Sloss), 95
Lilienthal, Samuel, 112
Lilienthal-Pratt House, 95; *94*
Locust Street, 95
Lombard Street, 169
Lord and Burnham, greenhouse mfrs., 86
Lotta's Fountain (Wyneken and Townsend), 120; *120*
Louise, queen of Denmark, 70
Lucas, Turner & Company, Bank of (Clark), 49; *48*
Lyon, Moses J.: Ohabai Shalome Temple, 128; *128*
Lyon Brewery, 190
Lyon Street, 189

McAllister Street, 130
McDougall, Charles and George: Calvary Presbyterian Church, 160; *160*
McElroy, William C., 34
McElroy Octagon House, 34; *35*
McKim, Mead & White, 19, 141, 192
McKinnon Avenue, 105
McLaren, John, 253, 264
McLaren Lodge, 253; *252–53*
McMorry, Farrell, 239
McMorry-Lagen House, 239; *238*
McMullen, John, 181
McMullen House, 181; *181*
Macondray, Capt. Frederick, 71
Madison Square Garden (New York), 141
Maiden Lane, 116
Malone, Jonathan, 14
Mansion Hotel (Mathews; Sawyer), 176; *176*
"Mansion Row," 182
mansions, 69, 106, 123, 126, 176, 182, 219, 285
Marist Fathers, 248
Market Street, 20, 23, 37, 120, 121, 126, 141, 144, 190, 193, 205, 215, 216, 222, 224, 228, 236
Market Street Railway Company: Fillmore Street Substation, 158; *158;* Spreckles Car House, 256; *256*
Mark Hopkins Hotel (Weeks and Day), 268; *269*
Martin, Camillo, 45
Masons: first meeting site, 27; theater, 25
Mason Street, 76, 263, 268, 273
Mastropasqua, Louis: Julius' Castle, 178; *179*
Mathews, Arthur, 170, 192, 198
Mathews, Lucia, 192
Mathews, J. C., and Son: Chambers Mansion, 176; *176*
Maybeck, Bernard, 141: Family Service Agency, 167; *166–67;* Palace of Fine Arts, 138; *138–39;* Roos House, 95; *94*
Mechanics Institute, 198
Medico-Dental Building, 30; *30*
Melodeon Theater, 27
Merrill, Frank, 124
Merrill Conservatory, 124; *125*
Metropolitan Life Insurance Company Building, 243; *243*
Mexican Land Grant of 1836, 111
Meyer, Frederick. *See* Meyer and O'Brien
Meyer, Joseph: Samuels Clock, 121; *121*
Meyer and O'Brien: Cadillac Hotel, 262; *262*
Meyers, Henry, 233
Middleton, John, and Sons, 58
mikvah, 175
Miller, Adam: Miller-Joost House, 126; *126*
Miller and Pflueger: Castro Theater, 154; *155;* San Francisco Mining Exchange, 170; *170;* Top of the Mark, 268
Miller-Joost House (Miller), 126; *126*
Mills, Darius Ogden, 19, 118, 170
Mills Building and Tower (Burnham and Root; Polk; Hobart), 12, 118; *119*
Minnesota Street, 196
Mish, Phenes and Sarah, 105
Mish House, 105, 136; *104*
Mission District, 111, 124, 175
Mission Dolores. *See* Mission San Francisco de Asis
Mission High School (1909), 182
mission house, 77
Mission San Francisco de Asis (Mission Dolores), 9, 17, 21; *16*
Mission Street, 20, 23, 63, 163
Mitsui Company, 244
MJB Coffee, 186, 227
modern buildings, 66, 116
Monterey Boulevard, 124
Montgomery Block office building, 10, 11

Montgomery Street, 10, 11, 12, 27, 28, 41, 49, 118, 164, 233, 289
monuments, 76, 146
Moore, Albert: Morgan House, 244; *245*
Mooser, William, Jr.: Haslett Warehouse, 101; *100*
Morgan, Frederick, 244
Morgan, Julia: Clay Street Center and Residence Club, 180; *180;* Potrero Hill Neighborhood House, 135; *134*
Morgan House (Pissis and Moore), 244; *245*
Morgan Oyster Company, 244
Moro, Jo, 170
Morris Store (Wright), 10, 12, 116; *117*
Moulanie Building, 49; *48*
Municipal Railway System, 256
Murphy, Edward, 169
Mustard Building, 54

Napier Lane houses, 9, 289
Nasser family, 154
National Historic Landmark, 106
National Historic Monuments, cable cars as, 76
National Register Historic District, 14, 130
National Register of Historic Places, 23, 86, 101, 106, 112, 120, 128, 147, 163, 296–97
National Trust for Historic Preservation, 112
Native American buildings, 9, 17
Neighborhood Conservation Studies, 14
Neoclassical Style, 128, 275
Neutra, Richard, 10
Newcomb Avenue, 25
New England influences, 111
Newman's Gym, 262
New Montgomery Street, 37, 234
Newsom, Samuel: Theodore Green Apothecary, 257; *257;* additions, John McMullen House, 181; *181*
Newsom brothers, 292
New St. Mary's Church, 18, 23
New York City, 11
New York Stock Exchange, 170
Nightingale, John, 81
Nightingale House, 81; *80–81*
19th Street, 175
Nob Hill, 106, 268
Noe Street, 194
Norman Style, 102, 109
North Beach, 189, 190
Northeast Waterfront Historic District, 14, 157, 289; *288*
North Point, 54
Notre Dame des Victoires Church and Rectory, 248; *249*
Notre Dame School, 202; *203*

Oakes Children's Center, 53; *53*
Oakley, William and Jenny, 278
Oakley Residence and Flats, 278

Oak Street, 58, 105, 136, 137
O'Brien, Smith. *See* Meyer and O'Brien
octagonal houses, 34, 65
Odd Fellows, 27
O'Doul, Francis "Lefty," Bridge (Strauss), 279; *279*
O'Farrell Street, 23, 72
Ohabai Shalome Temple (Lyon), 128; *128*
Old City Hall, 61, 81
Old French Consulate, 45; *45*
Old Holy Virgin Russian Orthodox Church, 53; *52*
Old Spaghetti Factory, 189
Old St. Mary's Church, 18, 20; *18*
Old St. Patrick's Church, 23; *22*
Old Transamerica Building (Paff), 89; *88*
Opera House. *See* War Memorial Opera House
Orick, Herrington, and Sutcliffe, Law Offices of (Kelham), 228; *228*
Oriental Warehouse, 13, 151; *150*
Orpheum Theater Building (Priteca), 144; *144–45*
Ortman-Shumate House, 153; *152*
Otis, James, 71

Pacific Avenue, 12, 78, 97, 271
Pacific Gas & Electric Company, 69; Jessie Street Substation (Polk), 13, 136; *8;* Station J, 204; *204*
Pacific Hardware and Steel Company (Sutton and Weeks), 278; *278*
Pacific Mail Steamship Company, 151, 289
Pacific Union Club (Laver; Polk), 106; *107*
Packard automobile showroom, 221
Paderewski, Ignace, 83
Paff, Charles: Banco Populare Italiano Operaia Fugazi, 89; *88*
Page Street, 83
Palace Hotel (Kelham), 23, 37, 234; *36–37*
Palace of Fine Arts (Maybeck), 138; *138–39*
Palace of the Legion of Honor, 285
Palou, Fr. Francisco, 17
Panama-California Exhibition (San Diego, 1915), 200
Panama-Pacific International Exposition (1915), 69, 121, 138, 253, 262, 291
Pantages Theater Building (Priteca), 144; *144–45*
Pantheon (Rome), 192
parish houses, 23, 177
Park Superintendent's Residence, 253; *252–53*
Parrott, John, 31
Patterson, Daniel J.: Southern Pacific Company Hospital Complex, 275; *274–75*
Pattigan, Haig, 192
Pelican Paper Company, 143; *142*
Percy, George W.: First Unitarian Church, 71; *71;* Kohl Building (with Willis Polk), 233; *232*

Percy and Hamilton: Sharon Building, 184; *184–85;* Trinity Presbyterian Church, 243; *242*
Petit Trianon, Le. *See* Koshland House
Phelan, James, 224
Phelan, James Duval, 291
Phelan Building, 193, 224; *225*
Phelps, Abner, House, 9, 58, 136; *59*
Phelps, Augusta, 58
Pierce, W., & Company, 28
Pierce Street, 85
Pine Street, 63, 153, 230
Pioneer Woolen Mill and D. Ghirardelli Company (Ghirardelli Square), 54; *54–55*
Piper, Stephen L., 102
Piper House, 102; *103*
Pissis, Albert, 292: Borel Building, 164; *164;* Flood Building, 216; *217;* Hibernia Bank, 190; *191;* Lane Library, 170; *171;* Morgan House, 244; *245*
playground facility, 184
Polk, Willis, 141: Beach Chalet, 267; *267;* Bourne Mansion, 69; *68;* Filoli, 69; Hallidie Building, 66, 222; *67;* Hobart Building, 236; *237;* Jessie Street Substation, 136; *8;* Kohl Building (with George W. Percy), 233; *232;* reconstructions and restorations: Atkinson House, 148; Flood Mansion (Pacific Union Club), 106; *107;* Mills Building, 118; *119;* Mission San Francisco de Asis, 17; *16*
Polk Street, 42, 200, 258
Portsmouth Plaza, 289
"Postcard Row," 198, 287
post office annex, 163
Post Street, 198, 222
Potrero Hill Neighborhood House (Morgan), 135; *134*
Potrero School, 196; *196*
Powell Street, 200, 216
Pratt, Orville C., Jr., 95
Presbyterian Church, 77, 135
Presbyterian Mission House, 77; *77*
Presidio, 95, 291
Priteca, B. Marcus: Pantages Theater Building, 144; *144–45*
Proposition M, 14
Public Library, 37

Queen Anne Style, 10, 93, 115, 123, 126, 176, 244, 270
Queen House (Brown; Van Trees), 285
Quinn, Mary, 105
Quinn House, 105

railroad buildings, 158, 169, 256
Ralston, William Chapman, 19, 31, 170
Real Estate Associates, 287
rectories, 177, 248, 255

Refregier, Anton, 163
Refugee Shack, 251; *251*
Reid, John, Jr.: Firehouse, Engine Company No. 8, 271; *271;* High School of Commerce, 200; *200*
Reid Brothers: Fairmont Hotel, 273; *272–73;* First Congregational Church, 263; *263*
residential hotel, 229
restaurants, 178, 205, 208, 211
Reuf, Abraham "Boss," 61, 201
Revere Avenue, 102
Richmond Masonic Lodge, 186
Rincon Annex Post Office (Underwood), 10, 163; *162*
Rincon Hill, 20
Riordan, Abp. Patrick, 219, 248
Ritz-Carlton Hotel, 243; *243*
Rolph, James, 291
Romanesque Revival Style, 72, 123, 184, 227, 255
Roosevelt, Franklin D., 267
Roos, Leon L., 95
Roos House (Maybeck), 95; *94*
Ross, T. Patterson: Islam Temple, 283; *282–83*
Roth, William Matson, 54
Rothchild, Henriette, 169
Rothchild, Hugo, 169
Rothchild House, 169
Rothenberg Early Childhood Center (Gutterson), 250; *250*
roundhouse, 169
Rousseau, Charles J., 115, 292
Royal Botanical Gardens (Kew, England), 86
Royal Globe Insurance Company Building, 230; *231*
Russian Club, 198
"Russian Consulate." *See* Westerfeld House
Russian Hill, 65, 79
Russian Orthodox Church, 53

Sacramento Street, 53, 77, 158, 170, 176, 204, 211, 285
St. Ansgar Danish Lutheran Church, 70; *70*
St. Boniface Church and Rectory, 255; *254*
St. Charles School, 197; *197*
St. Francis Lutheran Church, 70; *70*
St. Francis of Assisi Church, 21; *21*
St. James Episcopal Church, 132
St. John's Presbyterian Church (Dodge and Dolliver), 132; *132*
St. John the Baptist Parish, 23
St. Joseph's Church, Parish House, Rectory and Garden, 177; *177*
St. Mark's Evangelical Lutheran Church (Geilfuss), 72; *73*
St. Mary's Cathedral churches: Old St. Mary's, 18, 20; *18;* New St. Mary's, 18, 23, 219
St. Patrick's Church, 20, 23; *20. See also* Old St. Patrick's Church

St. Paulus Lutheran Church (Kraft), 172; *173*
St. Stephen's Episcopal Church, 53; *52*
Salfield and Kohlberg: Coleman House, 93; *92;* Sentinel Building, 61; *60*
Samuels, Albert S., Jewelry Company, 121
Samuels Clock (Samuels and Meyer), 121; *121*
San Carlos Street, 292
San Francisco Art Association, 133
San Francisco Art Institute (Bakewell and Brown), 133; *133*
San Francisco City and County Hospital, 186
San Francisco City Hall (Bakewell and Brown), 42, 130, 291; *43;* Rossi bust, 211. *See also* Old City Hall
San Francisco Civic Light Opera, 144
San Francisco Gas Light Company (Crockett), 98; *99*
San Francisco Jewish Community Center, Rothenberg Early Childhood Center, 250; *250*
San Francisco Landmarks Preservation Advisory Board, 11–15, 85, 288
San Francisco Mining Exchange (Miller and Pflueger), 170; *170*
San Francisco National Guard, 163
San Francisco Planning Commission, 205, 288, 293
San Francisco Redevelopment Agency, 12–13, 169
San Francisco Symphony, 37
San Francisco Women's Centers, 267
San Francisco Yacht Club, 182
San Jose Avenue, 256
San Miguel, Rancho, 126
San Simeon (Morgan), 180
Sansome Street, 63, 169, 228, 230
Savannah Street, 102
Savings Union Bank (Bliss and Faville), 192, 193; *192*
Sawyer, Houghton: alterations, Chambers Mansion, 176; *176*
Schilling Coffee, 227
Schmidt, Peter R.: Haas-Lilienthal House, 112; *113;* Stadmuller House, 63
Schmitz, Eugene, 215
Schoenstein Organ Building, 154; *154*
schools, 133, 196, 197, 200, 202
Schweinforth, A. C.: Ferry Building, 141; *140*
Schweitzer, Joseph, 190
Scott, Irving M., Primary School, 196; *196*
Scott Street, 153
Second Empire Style, 57, 81, 83, 182, 219, 280
Second Street, 236
Sentinel Building (Salfield and Kohlberg), 61; *60*
service agency buildings, 167, 250
Seventh Street, 278
Sharon, William, 184, 234
Sharon Building [office building], 234; *235*

Sharon Building [playground facility] (Percy and Hamilton), 184; *184–85*
Sheet Metal Workers Hall, 214; *215*
Sheppard-Dakin House, 79; *79*
Sheraton Palace Hotel. *See* Palace Hotel
Sherman, Leander S., 83
Sherman, William Tecumseh, 49, 289
Sherman, Clay & Company, 83
Sherman House (Sherman House Hotel), 83; *82*
Sherman's Bank. *See* Bank of Lucas, Turner & Company
Shingle Style, 10, 79, 243, 283
Shreve, George, 71
Shrine Temple, 283
Silver Dollar Saloon, 23
Sisters of the Holy Cross, 197
Sixth Street, 215
Skidmore, Owings & Merrill: Crown Zellerbach Complex and Site, 10, 260; *261*
skyscrapers, 61, 233, 236
Sloss, Louis, 95
Small, Dominic, 38
Society of California Pioneers, 81
Solari Buildings: East, 45; *44;* West, 45; *45*
South End Historic District, 291; *290*
Southern Pacific Company Hospital Complex (Patterson), 275; *274–75*
Southern Pacific Steamship Lines, 19
South San Francisco Opera House, 25; *24*
South Van Ness Avenue, 123, 182, 197
Spaghetti Factory, 189
Spanish Colonial Revival Style, 133, 167, 200, 229, 269
Spear Street, 163
Splendid Survivors (survey report), 13
Spreckles, Adolph and Alma, 285
Spreckles, John D., 256
Spreckles Car House, 256; *256*
Spreckles family, 189
Spreckles Mansion (Applegarth), 285; *284–85*
Spring Valley Water Company, 69, 97
stables, 28, 29
Stadmuller, Frederick D., 63
Stadmuller House (Schmidt), 13, 63
Stanford, Leland, 71
Stanyan, Charles, 111
Stanyan House, 9, 111; *111*
State Armory and Arsenal (Woollett and Woollett), 163; *163*
Steiner Street, 198, 287
Stevenson, Col. Jonathan, 289
Stevenson Street, 136
Stick Style, 10, 83, 95, 115, 123, 194, 198, 278
Stockton Street, 243
Stone, Frank M., 123
Stone House (Babson), 123; *122*
Story, William W.: Francis Scott Key Monument, 146; *146*

Strauss, J. B., 279; Third Street Bridge, 279; *279*
Streamline Moderne Style, 163
street-railway system: car house, 256; substation, 158
Sugar Palace. *See* Spreckles Mansion
Sullivan, Dennis T., 75
Sullivan Memorial Fire Chief's Residence, 75; *74*
Sumatra Street, 102
Sunnyside Conservatory, 124; *125*
Sunset District, 53
Sutro, Adolph Heinrich Joseph, 170
Sutter Street, 66, 175
Sutton and Weeks: Pacific Hardware and Steel Company, 278; *278*
Swain, Edward R., 141; Whittier Mansion, 123; *123*
Sylvester House, 102; *103*
synagogues, 128, 175

Tadich Grill, 208
Talbot, William C., 97
Talbot-Dutton House, 97; *96*
Tanforan Cottages, 111; *110*
Taylor Street, 79, 246
Telegraph Hill, 240, 289
Telegraph Hill Boulevard, 240
Telegraph Hill Historic District, 9, 10, 14, 289; *288*
Tenderloin District, 255, 262
Tennessee Street, 196
Tenth Avenue, 53
Tetrazzini, Luisa, 120
theaters, 25, 144, 154
theme groups, 14
Third Street Bridge (Strauss), 279; *279*
Tiffany, Louis, stained-glass windows, 109
Toklas, Alice B., birthplace, 15
Topke, William H., 292
Top of the Mark, 268
Touchard, Gustav, 248
towers, 54, 118, 141, 240
Transamerica Corporation, 89
transportation buildings, 141, 158, 169, 256
Tremont Hotel Building, 47; *46*
Tremont Stables, 29
Trinidad Bean and Elevator Company, 143; *142*

Trinity Episcopal Church (Brown), 109, 285; *108*
Trinity Presbyterian Church (Percy and Hamilton), 243; *242*
Trowbridge and Livingston, 37
Turk Street, 158
Turn Hall, 267; *266*
20th Street, 154
21st Street, 196
23rd Street, 243, 270
24th Avenue, 251
25th Street, 270
27th Avenue, 283

Underwood, Gilbert: Rincon Annex Post Office, 163; *162*
union hall, 215
Union Square, 12
Union Street, 34, 289
Union Trust Bank (Day), 192, 193; *193*
Unitarians, 71
United Nations, 130, 268
U.S. Mint and Subtreasury, 63; *62*
U.S. Post Office, Rincon Annex, 10, 163; *162*
U.S. Supreme Court, 11
University of Salamanca (Spain), 200
utility buildings, 98, 136, 201, 204

Vale, William, House, 244; *245*
Valencia Street, 292
Vallejo Street, 21, 57
Vandenburgh and Lewis, 270
Van Ness Avenue, 18, 23, 72, 130, 200, 220, 221
Van Trees, Frank S.: Koshland House, 147; *147*; Queen House, 285
Victorian styles, 10
Vigilante Movement, 289
Voz de Chile, La (newspaper), 27

Walter, Schilling & Company, 63
Ward, Clarence: Firehouse, Engine Company No. 37, 270; *270*
warehouses, 28, 101, 143, 151, 157, 278, 289, 291
War Memorial Opera House and Veterans

Building (Brown and Lansburgh), 130, 175, 291; *130–31*
Washington Street, 76, 137, 147, 285
Webster Street, 14, 69, 98, 287
Webster Street Historic District, 14, 287; *287*
Weeks and Day: Mark Hopkins Hotel, 268; *269*
Wells Fargo Bank Branch. *See* Union Trust Bank
Westerfeld, William, 198
Westerfeld House (Geilfuss), 198, 287; *199*
Western Addition, 13
Wharff, Edmund M.: Burr House, 57; *56*
Wheeler, James W., & Company, 33
Whistler-Patri: additions, Hills Brothers Coffee Building, 227
Whittier, William Franklin, 123
Whittier Mansion (Swain), 123; *123*
Wilbert, Fred, 214
Wilbert Blacksmith Shop, 214; *214*
Wilhelm, Kaiser, 258
windmill, 213
Wisconsin Street, 211
Women's Building, The, 267; *266*
Woodbridge, Sally and John, 260
Woollett and Woollett: State Armory and Arsenal, 163; *163*
World War II, 289
Wormser, Isaac, 91
Wormser-Coleman House, 91; *90*
WPA projects, 163, 267
Wright, Frank Lloyd: Morris Store, 10, 12, 116; *117*
Wurster, Bernardi, and Evans: Ghirardelli Square, *54–55*
Wyneken and Townsend: Lotta's Fountain, 120; *120*

Xenon's Hall, 27

Yeon Building, 47; *46*
Yerba Buena, 21, 289
Yerba Buena Center, 13

Zellerbach, Anthony, 260
Zellerbach, James David ("J. D."), 260
Zellerbach family, 189